WITH

THEIR EYES TURNED SKYWARD:

SANTA BARBARA'S FALLEN AVIATORS
OF
WORLD WAR II

―――◆―――

MICHEL NELLIS
Community Historian

and

KAREN RAMSDELL
Airport Director

JANAWAY PUBLISHING, INC.
Santa Maria, California
2012

Copyright © 2012 by Michel Nellis and Karen Ramsdell

ALL RIGHTS RESERVED. Written permission must be secured from the author or publisher to use or reproduce any part of this book, in any form or by any means, including electronic reproduction, except for brief quotations in critical reviews or articles.

Published by
Janaway Publishing, Inc.
732 Kelsey Ct.
Santa Maria, California 93454
(805) 925-1038
www.JanawayPublishing.com

2012

ISBN: 978-1-59641-251-4

Cover design by Janaway Publishing Inc.

Cover photograph of the P-38 Lightning aircraft courtesy of Planes of Fame Air Museum.

The quotations contained in the biographical section of Lieutenant Francis Frederick Hebel, pages 43-44, were reprinted, with the permission of the Naval Institute Press, from the book:
Lundstrom, John B. *The First Team: Pacific Naval Air Combat from Pearl Harbor to Midway.* Annapolis, Maryland: Naval Institute Press, 1984.

Made in the United States of America

*To the men and women of our Armed Forces
who made the ultimate sacrifice to preserve the freedoms
we enjoy today and so often take for granted*

CONTENTS

Contents v

Authors vii

Acknowledgements ix

Preface xi

Introduction xiii

Aviators:

    Adams, Lieutenant Clyde McAllister 2
    Arnold, Corporal Dean Alden 4
    Bates, Ensign Phillip Henry 6
    Becknell, Sergeant Wallace Earl 8
    Botello, Staff Sergeant Francis L 10
    Burns, Captain James Edward, Jr. 12
    Carman, Lieutenant Earnest Darrel 14
    Cass, Major Gerald M. 16
    Cook, Sergeant Cecil Palrang, Jr. 18
    Courville, Lieutenant Earl A. 20
    Coverstone, Lieutenant Robert E. 22
    Dibblee, Lieutenant Francis Richard 24
    Donaldson, Lieutenant John Louis 26
    Eckles, Lieutenant Rex Albert 28
    Firestone, Lieutenant Norman Selwyn 30
    Fowler, Lieutenant James Laurence 32
    Griggs, Lieutenant Augustus Monroe, Jr. 34
    Harshbarger, Captain William Miller 36
    Hartley, Lieutenant Cyril Owen 38
    Hays, Private John William 40
    Hebel, Lieutenant Francis Frederick 42
    Keister, Lieutenant Robert Louis 46
    Lopez, Lieutenant Frederick Peter 48
    Love, Lieutenant David Culver 50
    MacFarland, Lieutenant Andrew Ransalier 52
    Marxmiller, Staff Sergeant Robert K. 54
    McAllister, Lieutenant (j.g.) Earl Alder 56
    McCloskey, Lieutenant Fred Chadwick 58
    Mesa, Sergeant Nicholas John 60
    Miller, Staff Sergeant John Emil 62

Moffett, Lieutenant William Lynn 64
Mollenhauer, Ensign Arthur Paul 66
Moon, Aviation Cadet Felix Lee 68
Newman, Lieutenant Robert William 70
Oeschler, Lieutenant Richard, Jr. 72
Owens, Radioman Second Class William Thomas 74
Peck, Lieutenant Clifford Joseph 76
Peres, Lieutenant Jack 78
Rickard, Master Sergeant Jack B. 80
Roberts, Lieutenant Kenneth E. 82
Sawyer, Sergeant Clarence Robert, Jr. 84
Soto, Sergeant Stanley Howard 86
Stine, WASP Trainee Betty Pauline 88
Toms, Lieutenant George Parker, Jr. 90
Troup, Corporal John Robert 92
Verhelle, Lieutenant Edward George 94
Wade, Corporal Alan Laverne 96
Wilber, Lieutenant Dean Kent 98
Yee, Private Sam M. 100

Bibliography 103

Index 123

ABOUT THE AUTHORS

MICHEL NELLIS

A native Californian, Michel has always had a love for local history. She earned a B.A. degree in History from the University of California, Los Angeles, and a M.A. degree in Public Historical Studies at the University of California, Santa Barbara, with an emphasis in business history. Her thesis, *Profile of Downtown Isla Vista,* is a definitive study of the commercial area of this small enclave adjacent to the UC Santa Barbara campus.

She has researched and written about several areas of Santa Barbara County including the commercial area of Guadalupe, the rural areas of Lompoc Valley and Foxen Canyon, Santa Barbara's Mission Canyon district, the hedgerows of Montecito, northern Carpinteria Valley, and the tiny communities of Casmalia, Garey, and Sisquoc.

Besides history, Michel enjoys genealogy, travel adventures, and supporting a girls' school in Ghana, West Africa, through her non-profit, Women to Women International.

KAREN RAMSDELL

Karen was born in Los Angeles, California, and received her B.A. degree from the University of California, Santa Barbara, in 1971.

She held various positions with the City of Santa Barbara beginning in 1976 and is the Director of the Santa Barbara Airport, a position she has held since 1987. She directs the entire operation and maintenance of the airport, overseeing a $13 million budget. Karen is active in professional organizations that include the California Association of Airport Executives and the American Association of Airport Executives. In 2000, she was named Executive of the Year by the Southwest Chapter of the American Association of Airport Executives.

Karen's commitment and dedication to community issues is demonstrated by her membership in the Chambers of Commerce for Santa Barbara and the Goleta Valley. She also serves on the board of directors of the Goleta Valley Historical Society.

ACKNOWLEDGEMENTS

It goes without saying that an undertaking such as this requires the collaboration and contributions of many. Although the collection of information from various public records and other sources has been simplified and made easier with the advent of computers and the World Wide Web, research such as this still requires examining and scrutinizing books, manuscripts, files, and other material in search of relevant information. Fortunately, our task in this effort was made significantly easier with the many contributions by the Santa Barbara Public Library, the *Santa Barbara News Press*, Santa Barbara High School, and many other individuals and organizations.

And finally, a special note of appreciation is reserved for the family members who, through personal interviews, and the sharing of photographs, letters and other information, were able to provide us with invaluable information and material about their lost loved ones.

PREFACE

In May 2009, a handsome granite memorial was erected at the Santa Barbara Airport to honor those Santa Barbara aviators who lost their lives during World War II. Several hundred people attended the dedication ceremony not to glorify war, but to recognize the defining event of the 20th century and to pay tribute to a generation of Americans who made an overwhelming effort to preserve the freedoms we enjoy today and often take for granted.

I have been asked, "Why a memorial at the Santa Barbara Airport?" The airport has had a rich history dating back to the 1920s with World War II being one of its most significant periods. The airport today is not so different in appearance from what it was when the Marine Corps Air Station was hastily constructed there to train pilots to fly missions in the Pacific Theater. The airport's streets were originally identified by letters of the alphabet but were renamed after the war for local aviators who gave their lives during World War II.

About ten years ago, as the future of the airport was being planned, it became apparent that redevelopment would undoubtedly result in some of the airport streets being decommissioned and the names of these honored aviators would be forgotten. It was then that the idea for a memorial took root. The vision was two-fold: to create a permanent place to honor and recognize the local fallen aviators and to honor the Marine squadrons who served at the Marine Corps Air Station during the war.

At the time the Air Station construction was going full speed ahead, local men and women were enlisting in all branches of the Armed Forces. They left the lives of most young people – jobs, their first cars, their girlfriends, college applications. As many finished their education, local high school yearbooks captured their hopes and dreams: Betty Stine planned to become an airline stewardess after graduation; Earl Courville was to study electrical engineering; Rex Eckles wanted to enroll in an agricultural college; James Fowler would attend UCLA and then return to Santa Barbara to take up lemon ranching; Jack Peres hoped to become an army surgeon; and Frederick Lopez, like many young people his age, was undecided about what he wanted to do. They all gave up these opportunities to do the job they had been called to do. But they didn't come back. Two hundred sixty-four residents from Santa Barbara County lost their lives during the war, forty-nine were aviators.

This volume immortalizes the sacrifices that these forty-eight men and one woman made to help ensure the safety and freedom of Americans down through the generations. It has been an honor to help write their stories.

Karen Ramsdell
Santa Barbara, California
February 15, 2012

INTRODUCTION

"There is a mysterious cycle in human events. To some generations much is given. Of other generations much is expected. This generation of Americans has a rendezvous with destiny."

These words were spoken by President Franklin D. Roosevelt when he addressed the Democratic National Convention in 1936 at a time when the nation was dealing with the Great Depression. How prophetic as only five years later this generation of Americans would be called upon to sacrifice once again as the United States entered the Second World War.

During World War II, sixteen million Americans served in the Armed Forces. Local young people also answered the call to duty and put their lives on hold – foregoing college, marriage, jobs. By the war's end, there were one million American casualties and over 400,000 dead. In Santa Barbara County, 264 died in service to their country including forty-nine aviators whose service and lives are honored on the Santa Barbara Airport World War II Memorial.

While most of the aviators grew up on the south coast and attended local high schools, a few had connections to the area through family members or spouses. James Burns met his future wife, Mary Ellen Putnam, at the USO in Bakersfield. She had graduated from Santa Barbara High School in 1939 along with aviators Edward Verhelle, Cyril Hartley, James Fowler, Norman Firestone, and Betty Stine. Earnest Carman, another aviator, never lived in Santa Barbara; however, his mother, Clara Starr Carman, spent her youth here. William Moffett followed his brother Leonard from Idaho to attend college in Santa Barbara.

Most of the aviators attended either Santa Barbara or Carpinteria High School and were active in sports, student government, and ROTC. Almost half of them pursued college before entering the service. Thirty-nine served with the Army Air Corps, four were Marines, and six were Navy men. Though most served in the Asian and Pacific Theaters, others saw combat in Europe and the Mediterranean.

The oldest honored aviator was Sam Yee, born approximately 1909 in China where he left a wife and son to work in California. He enlisted in 1942; his story is brief as little could be uncovered as to the circumstances of his service to his adopted country. John Hays was another older enlistee who became a paratrooper at the age of thirty-two and served in the South Pacific. The youngest flier was Felix Moon Jr. who actually did not join the Armed Services until 1946 when he was eighteen. Though he did not see war action, the Santa Barbara City Council deemed it appropriate to honor him after he died in a training accident in 1949.

The highest ranking aviator honored was Major Gerald Cass who had been a court stenographer in Santa Barbara's Superior Court before enlisting in the Army Air Corps a month after the bombing of Pearl Harbor. Ironically, while on his last mission in the South Pacific, he was promoted from Captain to Major but died in combat never learning of his new rank.

With Their Eyes Turned Skyward

The aviators either flew or were assigned to a variety of aircraft including single-pilot planes such as the P-38 Lightning and the P-51 Mustang or heavy bombers carrying crews of nine men or more. Lieutenant Dean Wilber trained in the Taylorcraft Grasshopper which was used as an American observation and liaison aircraft much as the French used air balloons for reconnaissance. Navy Lieutenant Francis Hebel flew the F4F Wildcat, one of the first monoplanes to fly from U.S. carrier flight decks.

Not all aviators were pilots or co-pilots. Some served as navigators; others as bombardiers and gunners. Jack Rickard was a mechanic, three were radio operators, and Nick Mesa was an aerial photographer. Two were paratroopers.

Nine of the aviators died stateside. Captain William Harshbarger completed his tour of duty and was assigned as a flight instructor on the B-24. On one of its training missions in the summer of 1944, the plane crashed near Walla Walla, Washington, killing all eight crew members. Corporal Alan Wade also died in a plane crash near Walla Walla the same year. Cadets Betty Stine and Felix Moon, Ensign Philip Bates, Lieutenants Clyde Adams, Augustus Griggs, and Cyril Hartley were all killed in domestic aircraft training accidents. Lieutenant Earl Courville died in an automobile accident five miles from his base in North Carolina.

Other Santa Barbara fliers died either in combat, in air collision accidents, or as a result of mechanical failure. Sergeant Cecil Cook and Lieutenant Robert Newman died as prisoners of war of the Japanese. Sergeant Cook was aboard a Japanese POW boat that was bombed by unsuspecting Allied planes. Lieutenant Newman was a victim of a fierce shelling by the Japanese in the Philippines.

A surprising number of the aviators were married and left widows and orphans. Paratrooper John Hays had two sons, one old enough to remember the last time he saw his dad. Other servicemen never met their offspring. Andy MacFarland was born four months after his father, Lieutenant Andrew MacFarland, was killed. That same month Kathleen was born just two months after her father, Lieutenant Richard Oeschler, was killed in a crash landing in the China Sea.

Many American families had more than one child serving in the military and Santa Barbara families were no exception. Fifteen of the fliers had siblings who served somewhere in the Armed Services. Clara Starr Carman was proud of the fact that she had four sons in uniform and three daughters working for the war effort. Sergeant Stanley Soto was one of three brothers to enlist. His brother Bernard joined the army and was later captured by the Japanese and died in a Philippines prison camp. Younger brother Francis also enlisted in the Army, but when Marine Staff Sergeant Stanley Soto was killed, Francis was relieved from combat duty and permanently assigned stateside duties. A War Department policy stated that the sole surviving son of a family who lost two or more sons in the service of their country could not serve overseas.

Sixty-six years have passed since the close of World War II. Each day more and more veterans of this global conflict slip away and soon their stories will be forgotten. The authors of the following biographies were determined not to allow the same fate for the forty-nine aviators honored on the Santa Barbara Airport Memorial. It took eighteen months to research, interview, and write their stories.

Family members contacted were both surprised and delighted that someone cared enough to remember their loved ones. John Mesa sent photos of his dad, Sergeant Nick Mesa, along with images of the patches he once wore. Kathy Oeschler Shanalec entrusted her only photos of her father to the U.S. Mail to be included in this volume. Dale McAllister and his wife drove from Utah the summer of 2009 to share photos and memories of his brother, Lieutenant (j.g.) Earl McAllister. Wilda Irvine produced letters and photographs of her two service brothers, George and John Donaldson, as did Irma Nagelmann about her brother, Lieutenant Edward Verhelle, and Mary Alice Coffman about her uncle, Lieutenant Francis Hebel, Santa Barbara County's first war casualty.

Besides personal interviews, other resources used included books, internet sites, and newspaper articles which took nearly four months to peruse and scan. The quality of some of the photographs has been compromised because of the age of the documents used. Facts have been verified as much as humanly possible.

Aviation changed forever the way war is fought; once America entered the Second World War, aircraft factories produced almost 100,000 planes per year. Planes were used to drop bombs, act as escorts, carry people and equipment, and conduct reconnaissance. Air war was the key in so many battles especially in the Pacific Theater. Each of these aviators had a stake in winning the war from on high and, like da Vinci, kept their eyes turned skyward. They never really did return to Earth.

> *"Those who have tasted flight will walk the Earth with their eyes turned skyward, for there they have been and there they long to return."*
> Leonardo da Vinci

AVIATORS

LIEUTENANT CLYDE MCALLISTER ADAMS

Clyde Adams discovered his passion for aviation when he was just a teenager. So it is not surprising that when he enlisted in the military, he chose to train as a pilot.

Clyde was born in Ventura on August 28, 1921, the only child of Claude McAllister and Lillian Sophia Adams. The family moved to Santa Barbara when he was about seven years old and then to Hawaii when Clyde was ten years old. In Hawaii, Clyde earned his pilot's license at the age of sixteen. Three years later, he enlisted in the Canadian Air Force and trained in Canada for eight months. After the Japanese attacked Pearl Harbor, he enlisted from Hawaii in the American Air Force. He trained at Williams Field in Arizona as a bomber pilot where he earned his wings and his commission as a lieutenant. Williams, the Air Force's Advanced Flying School and foremost pilot training facility, graduated more pilots and instructors than any base in the country.

Lt. Clyde M. Adams

Clyde was the archetypical fighter pilot, flying fast and alone in his P-38 Lightning aircraft. This fighter plane was first produced in 1939 by Lockheed and was used throughout World War II. The Germans nicknamed it "fork-tailed devil," and the Japanese called it "two planes, one pilot" because of its distinctive design of twin booms and a single nacelle containing the cockpit and war equipment. The plane was used in different roles including dive bombing, level bombing, ground strafing, photo reconnaissance, and as a long-range escort fighter. It was used most successfully in the Pacific Theater.

The P-38 Lightning, a fighter aircraft, similar to the one used by Lieutenant Clyde McAllister Adams

From Williams Field, Clyde transferred to Eglin Field in Florida. Eglin was originally established as an armament and gunnery base in the 1930s and became an important armaments testing facility for the Army Air Force during World War II. In April 1942, it became a Proving Ground Command Post for operational tests and studies of aircraft and airborne equipment.

On May 2, 1943, Lieutenant Adams took off from Eglin Field in a P-38G-12-LO on a simulated, minimum altitude, ground strafing mission. He repeatedly dove over the Gulf of Mexico while firing machine guns and a cannon. Apparently while practicing, he misjudged his altitude and the plane hit the water. The search and rescue team found an oil slick, and divers located only pieces of the wreckage and a small portion of his body.

Santa Barbara's Fallen Aviators of World War II

After Clyde's death, his parents received a letter from his commanding officer, Major Henry B. Darling, praising the young man:

> *"Clyde was held in high esteem by all members of the command. He was one of our finest pilots and his loss will be an irreplaceable one to a fighting organization of the air forces. In addition to his qualities as a pilot, he was a brilliant, popular officer and a gentleman. He will leave many friends who will never forget his ideal qualities as an officer, pilot and friend. Lieutenant Adams lost his life honorably in the service of his country. I feel there can be no finer obituary."*

Funeral services for Lieutenant Adams were held May 17, 1943, at Trinity Episcopal Church in Santa Barbara. A Guard of Honor brought his remains home escorted by a fellow officer of the lieutenant. His body was interred at the Santa Barbara Cemetery.

Clyde's parents remained in Santa Barbara and later in life operated Adams Refinishing Shop. Both Claude and Lillian lived to be almost ninety. After their deaths, they were buried alongside their beloved son. In 1948, the streets surrounding the Santa Barbara Airport were named for local aviators who lost their lives during World War II. Clyde Adams Road is named for this young aviator.

Lt. Clyde McAllister Adams was killed on May 2, 1943, and was interred at Santa Barbara Cemetery on May 17, 1943

Flight Over Mexico Gulf Fatal to Pilot

Funeral services for Pilot Lieutenant Clyde M. Adams, killed in a plane crash in a flight over the Gulf of Mexico during a P-38 gun test mission nearly two weeks ago, will be held Monday at 11 a.m. in Trinity Episcopal church. A guard of honor will bring his remains to Santa Barbara today, the escort being a fellow officer, Lieutenant James C. Austin of Eglin field, Fla. He was the son of Mr. and Mrs. C. M. Adams, 2009 Monterey avenue.

The lieutenant, a native of Ventura, was 22. He enlisted in the Canadian air force in 1941 and trained eight months in Canada. After Pearl Harbor he transferred to the American Air forces and received his wings and commission at Williams field, Ariz.

Since then he has been stationed at Eglin field. Lieutenant Adams started his flying career when he was only 16 and lived in Hawaii with his parents. It was there he took his first solo flight and earned his private pilot's license.

PRAISED BY OFFICER

His commanding officer, Major Henry B. Darling, in a letter to the pilot's family praised the youth.

"You have the deepest sympathy of the officers and men of this organization in your bereavement," he wrote. "Clyde was held in high esteem by all members of the command. He was one of our finest pilots and his loss will be an irreplaceable one to a fighting organization of the air forces.

"In addition to his qualities as a pilot, he was a brilliant, popular officer and gentleman. He will leave many friends who will never forget his ideal qualities as an officer, pilot and friend. Lieutenant Adams lost his life honorably in the service of his country. I feel there can be no finer obituary."

Santa Barbara News Press,
May 16, 1943

CORPORAL DEAN ALDEN ARNOLD

Dean was born in Lone Tree, Missouri, in 1917, the third child of Price Younger and Ethel Mae Arnold. The family moved to Santa Barbara prior to the birth of their youngest son, Kenneth, in 1920. Dean attended local schools and graduated from Santa Barbara High School in 1935. The school yearbook noted that he had an interest in aviation though, following graduation, he went to work for City Meat Market.

In February 1942, Dean enlisted out of the city of Detroit where he was working as a buyer for a meat wholesale firm. His original intention was to become a medic; he was first trained at Will Rogers Field in Oklahoma. In September, he reported for pre-flight training as an aviation cadet in Santa Ana, California. Santa Ana was where aspiring cadets were tested for aptitudes and classified as pilots, navigators, or bombardiers. It was the only base to provide pre-flight training for all three classifications.

Cpl. Dean A. Arnold

Dean became a radio operator and was assigned to the 29th Bomber Group. The 29th had been activated in 1940 in Langley, Virginia, with four squadrons, including the 43rd to which Dean was assigned. After training at Langley, the bomber group moved to MacDill Field, Florida, and then to Govern Field, Idaho, for combat training. More training followed in Pratt, Kansas, where Dean completed his training in February 1945. The 29th Bomber Group was sent to Guam using B-29 aircraft. The B-29 Superfortress was built by Boeing and was the largest bomber to enter service in World War II. It was used only in the Pacific, and two of these planes carried the bombs dropped over Hiroshima and Nagasaki in August 1945.

B-29 Superfortress

The 29th Bomber Group flew sixty-six combat missions including both day and night raids between February 25 and August 15, 1945. They also engaged in air-sea rescue, weather reconnaissance, and radar scoping. The targets varied from airfields to aircraft factories, chemical plants, oil refineries, or industrial areas.

One of the Group's missions was to be Dean Arnold's last. Late on the night of March 9, 1945, and continuing into the early hours of the 10th, 279 bombers departed Guam on an assignment with the code name of "Operation Meetinghouse." Its purpose was to drop incendiary bombs on Tokyo, Japan's capital. One of the planes, captained by John L. Musser, took off from North Field Guam with a crew of eleven, including Corporal Arnold. The skies were clear and the visibility was unrestricted. The plane was last seen that morning at 2:10; what happened next was not immediately known. The plane and crew were declared missing the next day. The War Department later stated that the plane was shot down over Tokyo and no one survived.

43d Bombardment

Corporal Dean Arnold was memorialized at Jefferson Barracks National Cemetery in St. Louis, Missouri. His younger brother, Kenneth, also served during World War II as an aviation mechanic and returned home safely.

In 1948, the streets at the Santa Barbara Airport were named for local aviators who died during World War II. Dean Arnold Place bears the name of this courageous young man. Dean is also honored on the World War II Memorial at Santa Barbara High School.

Group Grave Marker for Corporal Dean Arnold and other crew members, Jefferson Barracks National Cemetery, St. Louis, Missouri

ENSIGN PHILLIP HENRY BATES

Philip Henry Bates was born in Santa Barbara on July 11, 1918, the middle of five children born to Thomas Wheatley and Bertha Lee Bates. Apparently the marriage did not last, and Philip was raised by his mother in Carpinteria. After graduating from Carpinteria High School, he enrolled at Occidental College in Los Angeles and graduated with a bachelor's degree.

Philip enlisted in the Navy in the spring of 1941 following in the footsteps of his two brothers, Kenneth and Fred. The Army drafted Kenneth, while Fred served as a flight instructor at the Long Beach Naval Station. Was it a happy coincidence that Philip received his preliminary aeronautical training in Long Beach?

Photo courtesy of Eric Swenumsen

Ensign Philip Henry Bates

Philip earned his wings in March 1942 and was then sent to Jacksonville, Florida, to train aviation cadets. Four months later near Jacksonville, while at the controls of his training plane with his trainee Remsen H. R. Crego on board, Ensign Bates's plane collided with another trainer carrying an instructor and his student. All four men were killed. Just before he was killed, Ensign Bates was in line to receive the Cutler Gold Wings for attaining the best grades in his class. The award was made posthumously.

A military funeral was held for Ensign Bates at the Carpinteria Community Church on July 20, 1942. His body had been brought from Florida accompanied by Ensign A. MacDougall.

Both of Philip's brothers survived the war as did a brother-in-law. Philip was the only family member to serve who did not return home alive. He was buried in the Carpinteria Cemetery with full military honors.

Santa Barbara's Fallen Aviators of World War II

Photograph courtesy of Eric Swenumsen (Nephew)
Ensign Philip Bates

SERGEANT WALLACE EARL BECKNELL

Known as Earl, Wallace Earl Becknell was born in 1913 in Hunt, Texas, and was raised in McKinney, Texas, deep in the heart of cotton country. Earl's younger brother Herman remembers that Earl loved to paint pictures and create signs. Herman considered his older brother very smart. The boys enjoyed hunting and fishing with their dad.

Earl graduated from Farmersville (Texas) High School. Years later the school erected a memorial to those students, including Earl, who lost their lives in the cause of war.

After high school, Earl enrolled at East Texas State Teachers College where he completed two semesters of course work before leaving school. He went to work for his grandfather operating the cotton gin as his brothers also did after finishing high school.

In 1937, Earl decided to strike out on his own and travelled to California. There he found work in the grocery business taking a job with Smart & Final in Santa Barbara. Along the way, he met Edna Mae Clark and married her in Santa Barbara the summer of 1939. She had a son Harry Eugene, who, according to Herman, Earl adopted.

Photo courtesy of Wendy Lensik
Sergeant Wallace Becknell

In October 1942, Earl enlisted in the army in Los Angeles and signed on with the Army Air Force. He trained as a waist gunner and was assigned to the Boeing B-17 Flying Fortress, a four-engine heavy bomber aircraft developed for the Army Air Force. The B-17 is considered the most important heavy bomber for the American allies in World War II flying in excess of 290,000 sorties over ground installations. It was used primarily in the daytime to bomb German industrial, civilian, and military targets.

Photograph courtesy of Sherry Shelton
358th Bomber Squadron. Sergeant Becknell, back row, fourth from left

Earl was attached to a crew captained by Gerald A. White. The crew of ten nicknamed their plane *Caught in the Draft*. As part of the 358th squadron, they were assigned to the 303rd Bomber Group (Heavy) of the 8th Air Force in January 1943. Known as the Hell's Angels, they trained in the United States. A year later, they were sent overseas and stationed at Molesworth, near Kettering, England. By now, Earl had attained the rank of sergeant.

It is likely that Sergeant Becknell's squadron was sent to Molesworth to help replace the nine aircraft and crew who had been lost on a bombing mission five days earlier on January 11, 1944. Their first mission over Bois Coquerel, France, was uneventful and no casualties occurred. On January 29, one plane was lost during a raid over Frankfurt, and the following day, all

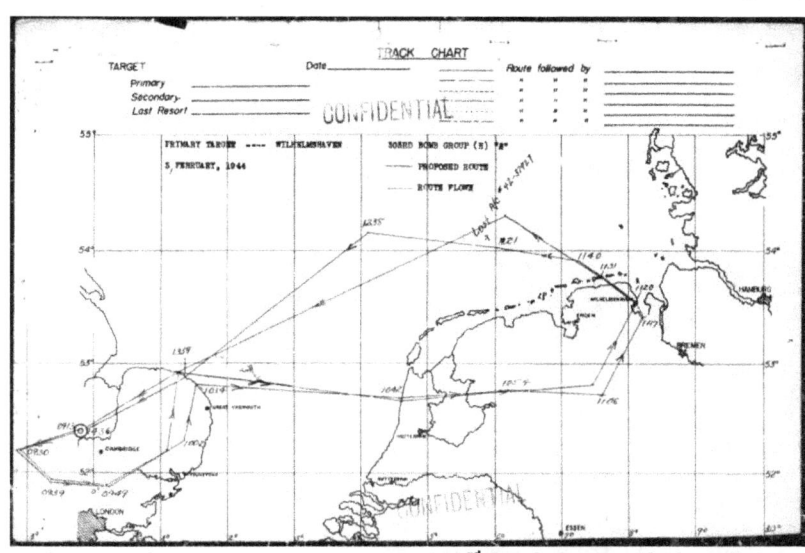

U. S. Army Air Force. War Department, 303rd Bomb Group, Missing Air Crew Report #A/C42-37927, February 3, 1944

planes returned safely from their mission over Brunswick, Germany. However, on their fourth mission, February 3, 1944, the entire crew of *Caught in the Draft* perished after a successful raid over Wilhelmshaven, Germany.

That day, *Caught in the Draft,* along with 800 bombers and accompanying fighters, left from Molesworth to bomb the U-Boat facilities and naval base at Wilhelmshaven. After the bombers hit their targets, they encountered overcast weather on the return trip to England. Captain White decided to cut away from the formation, perhaps looking for better visibility. Suddenly the plane rolled over on its back and headed straight down. It crashed into the North Sea and the entire crew of ten men was reported missing.

No bodies were recovered. However, Earl is memorialized on the Wall of the Missing in the American Cemetery in Margraten, Netherlands. A grave marker was erected in his memory in the Caddo Mills Cemetery in Texas. He was awarded the Air Medal and Purple Heart for his service. In 1948, the streets at the Santa Barbara Airport were named for local aviators who died during World War II, and Earl was honored with a street named for him. He was survived by his wife Edna Mae who died on January 3, 2008, in Santa Maria, California.

Sergeant Becknell is memorialized on the Wall of the Missing, American Cemetery, Margraten, Netherlands

STAFF SERGEANT FRANCIS L. BOTELLO

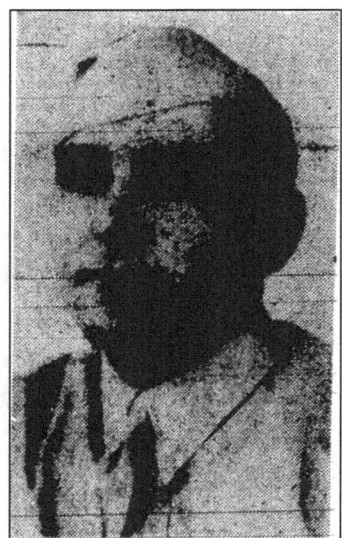

STAFF SERGEANT BOTELLO
Missing In Action

Sergeant Botello Lost in Romania

Staff Sergeant Francis Botello, U.S. Army Air Forces, has been reported missing in action over Romania, according to word received here by his wife and parents, Mrs. Virginia Botello, 817 Olive street, and Mr. and Mrs. M. A. Botello, 1724 State street.

The notification from the War Department said the staff sergeant failed to return after a bombing mission on May 5.

Santa Barbara News Press, May 25, 1944

Francis L. Botello and his younger siblings were descendants of long-time California families. Francis was born in Carpinteria on August 17, 1917, to Maclovio and Erlinda Botello. Maclovio managed the family ranch where he and Erlinda raised their children. In his later years, they moved into Santa Barbara where he worked as a fireman.

Francis finished three years of high school, then worked as a farm laborer before he enlisted in the National Guard at age twenty-three. He re-enlisted April 2, 1943, and joined the Army. The following year he married Virginia and together they lived in downtown Santa Barbara.

He graduated from Lowry Field in Colorado after receiving gunnery training as a crew member for both the B-17 and the B-24. The B-17 was first built in the late 1930s and was used extensively by the Army Air Force in daylight bombing campaigns against German targets. It was a potent and high-flying long-range bomber capable of great destruction and able to withstand extensive battle damage. The B-24 Liberator was also a heavy bomber of a more modern design with a longer range and could carry a heavier bomb load. However, it was more difficult to fly and prone to catching on fire. With its slab-like design, it earned the nickname "Flying Boxcar."

After training, Sergeant Botello was assigned to the 456th Bombardment Group of the 15th Air Force and sent to Europe as a member of the 745th Squadron based at Stornara Field, Italy. The 456th operated B-24 Liberators and was known unofficially as "Steed's Flying Colts," after its commander, Colonel Thomas W. Steed.

The Bomb Group flew its first combat mission in February 1944, less than two weeks after reaching Italy. All told, the 456th Bomb Group flew 249 bombing missions earning two Presidential Unit Citations for valor in combat.

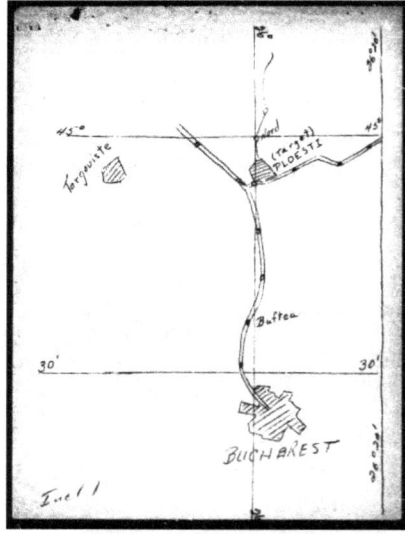

U.S. Army Air Force. War Department Missing Air Crew Report # 4749, May 10, 1944

The 456th participated extensively in the strategic bombing campaign against oil production targets held by the Axis powers. One important target was the oil refineries in Ploesti, Romania, where they repeatedly suffered extensive losses. On May 5, 1944, the 456th made the first of ten attacks on the Ploesti oil facilities losing three aircraft that day. Francis was the armament gunner on the B-24 Liberator *Taboo* on this bombing mission over

Ploesti. The plane with ten crew members on board was piloted by First Lieutenant Lawrence Peterson. The attack on Ploesti was of major importance, costing many American and Allied lives, but it was pivotal in stopping the Nazi war machine access to the oil refineries.

A B-24D Liberator, the *Taboo*, goes down over Ploesti. The aircraft was not hit by flak, but was mortally wounded when the body of a crewman from another B-24D struck the wingtip and broke off the outer wing panel! Of the 164 Liberators that attacked Ploesti, fifty-three failed to return. A much better loss ratio than had been predicted.

When *Taboo's* squadron reached the target, it ran into intense, accurate flak. Another aircraft in the formation was hit by the flak and the crew began to parachute out of the plane. One of the men hit the *Taboo* breaking off about ten feet of its wing. The plane went into a flat spin and went down. Two of the ten crew members were able to parachute to safety. Staff Sergeant Botello did not survive the crash.

Sergeant Botello and his fellow crew members are listed on a grave marker at the Jefferson Barracks in St. Louis, Missouri. A street at the Santa Barbara Airport is also named for him. He was survived by his parents and his wife.

CAPTAIN JAMES EDWARD BURNS, JR.

Known as Edward, Lieutenant Burns was born in El Centro in 1916. He was a UCLA graduate before joining the Army Air Corps in December 1940. His goal when he joined the military was to be an officer which he achieved when he made captain and became a flight instructor in Sioux City, Iowa.

In 1944, he was assigned to the 19th Bomb Group as a pilot of the B-29 dubbed the *Katie Ann* after his newly-born daughter. The B-29 or Flying Superfortress was the largest bomber to enter service in World War II and was used only in the Pacific. It later carried the atomic bombs dropped over Hiroshima and Nagasaki.

Captain Burns and the *Katie Ann* were attached to the 30th Bomb Squadron stationed on the island of Guam. While based there, he earned the Distinguished Flying Cross for successfully carrying out airstrikes over Japanese territory.

Events played out differently late on the night of April 13, 1945. Six B-29 bombers, including Captain Burns's plane, carrying sixty crew members were sent out on night raids headed for Tokyo. Three planes took off from Saipan, two from Guam, and one from Tinian, all in the Mariana Islands. Edward's plane was not seen after taking off from Guam's North Field nor was it in radio contact (radio silence was required unless an emergency had occurred).

Capt. James E. Burns, Jr.

Mary Ellen Putnam, wife of Captain James Burns, Jr.

The next day all six planes were reported missing, Captain Burns's plane among them with his crew of ten. Their mission was to have taken them over Tokyo on April 14 at 1:00 a.m. Instead the bombers encountered intense flak, a few enemy fighters, and numerous searchlights. Two of the planes were lost over the city of Tokyo, while the others were considered missing. In April 1946, all of the crew members were declared killed in action except for one member from another crew who did survive.

Captain Burns's widow, Mary Ellen, was notified of her husband's death by a phone call from an army officer. At the time she was living with her young daughter and her parents on East Arrellaga Street in Santa Barbara and working as a substitute teacher.

For his bravery and service, the late Captain Burns was awarded the Purple Heart, the Asia-Pacific Campaign and American Defense Medals. Mary Ellen also received his Distinguished Flying Cross with the following citation:

"For extraordinary achievement while participating in historical missions against the homeland of Japan between 9 March 1945 and 19 March 1945. Aircraft on each mission attacked these Japanese cities at precedent-shattering low altitudes, introducing new and successful tactics with devastating results.

"Each flight was made without regard to personal safety in the face of ever present danger from enemy fighters and heavy directed flak. These missions were flown over excessively long ranges through weather that was often adverse and necessitated instrument flying and increased navigational problems. There were ever present the possibility of mechanical failure and a failure due to enemy action, necessitating subsequent ditching many miles at sea in hostile waters.

"The rapid succession in which each mission followed the other allowed minimum time for rest and recuperation. In spite of weariness and fatigue, physical and mental strain, and the hazardous flying conditions, this individual displayed such courage and skill as to reflect great credit on himself and the Army Air Force."

Burns, Commander Of 'Santa Barbara' Superfort, Missing

Mrs. James Edward Burns Jr., 410 E. Arrellaga St., has been notified by the War Department that her husband, Capt. Burns, has been missing in action over Guam since April 14. At the time he was reported missing, he was on a mission over Tokyo as commander of his B-29 Superfortress, the "City of Santa Barbara."

Capt. Burns graduated from the University of California at Los Angeles in 1939 and entered the Army as a flying cadet in December, 1940. He received his commission eight months later, and served as instructor at Minter Field. Other posts in the State at which he served were at New Mexico, Iowa and Kansas.

The missing officer recently was awarded the Distinguished Flying Cross for missions over Japanese territory from March 9 to 19.

Mrs. Burns, the former Mary Ellen Putman, with their 14-months-old daughter, Kathryn Ann, resides here with her parents, Mr. and Mrs. Charles C. Putman. Capt. Burns' father, James E. Burns, is a resident of El Centro.

Santa Barbara News Press, May 20, 1945

Mary Ellen married again in 1946. She wed William DuBois, her husband's childhood friend from El Centro. They had three children and Bill also raised Katie as his own. A street at the Santa Barbara Airport is named in honor of Captain Burns. In 2004, when the World War II Memorial was dedicated in Washington DC, William and Mary Ellen Dubois honored Edward by listing him on the National Memorial Registry of Remembrances for his role as a commanding officer of his B-29.

LIEUTENANT EARNEST DARREL CARMAN

Lt. Earnest D. Carman

A Lassen County native, Lieutenant Carman was born February 16, 1920, to Elbert Levi and Clara Starr Carman. While attending Lassen High School, Earnest enjoyed acting. After high school, he enrolled in Lassen Junior College where he was elected president of the school's Alpine Club. He had completed two years of college when the United States entered World War II. He joined the Army Air Corps two days after the Japanese bombed Pearl Harbor.

In the Air Corps, Earnest attained the rank of second lieutenant and learned to fly the B-24 Liberator, an American-designed heavy bomber. It was produced in greater numbers than any other American combat aircraft of World War II. Often compared to the B-17 Flying Fortress, the Liberator was more modern, reached top speeds more quickly, and could carry a heavier bomb load. However, it was more difficult to fly and had a tendency to catch fire.

After earning his pilot's wings, Lieutenant Carman was assigned to the 837th Bomber Squadron of the 487th Heavy Bomber Group. Known as the "Gentlemen from Hell," the 487th was first activated in September 1943 at Bruning Army Airfield in Nebraska. After a series of hops both in the US and overseas, the bomber group finally arrived in Lavenham, England, in April 1944. Noteworthy was the fact that through all of the training and travel, no casualties were sustained by either air or ground personnel.

The B-24 Liberator, an American heavy bomber, similar to the one flown by Lt. Earnest Carman

On May 7, 1944, the 487th participated in its first combat mission over Liege, Belgium. On May 11, the bomber group suffered its first casualties when three aircraft were lost; among the personnel missing was the group commander. Then on May 20, thirty-six Liberators took off from Lavenham Airfield to again bomb Liege. At the control of one of these planes was Lieutenant Everett F. Goethe. His co-pilot was Second Lieutenant Earnest Carman. The plane carried eight other crew members.

As the plane climbed after take-off, it shuddered and started to fall back. The pilot tried to pull the plane up but the number two engine failed and the plane smashed into a grove of trees. The gasoline tanks exploded and the plane burst into flames. Shortly after the plane came to rest, at least one of the twelve 500-pound bombs the plane was carrying exploded.

A local police sergeant heard the crash and drove quickly to the scene of the accident. Since one bomb on board had already exploded, there was fear that more would soon. The police officer found one man lying on the ground with his clothes and body on fire. With help from nearby civilians, they cut off his clothes and carried him to safety. Another crew member was found dazed and injured but he survived. Lieutenant Carman was not so lucky; he and five other crewmen died that day.

Second Lieutenant Earnest D. Carman was buried in the American Cemetery in Cambridge, England. He was awarded the Purple Heart for his bravery. In 1963, the British Ministry of Defense was still concerned about the threat of danger at the crash site and refused requests to recover the remains of the bomber for museum display. Ammunition and aircraft fragments still reside in the woodlands of Long Melford, a grim reminder that both lives and equipment were lost at the hands of the enemy.

Lieutenant Carman's ties to Santa Barbara were through his mother. Clara had lived in the city as a child and returned after she divorced Elbert. In a newspaper interview before Earnest died, Clara stated how proud she was to have had four sons in uniform and three daughters who were working for the war effort. Lieutenant Carman was also survived by his wife Violet and their 10-month-old son.

Lt. Earnest Carman's grave, located in the American Cemetery, Cambridge, England

MAJOR GERALD M. CASS

Major Gerald M. Cass

Born in 1916, Gerald was the youngest of nine children born to Emery and Helen Cass. The family lived in tiny Collyer, Kansas, before moving to Gove County, slightly west and south of Collyer.

As a young man, Gerald met and married Edna Grace Kurtz. They had a daughter, Ruth Helen, born in February 1936. The marriage did not last long and the couple divorced.

Gerald left Kansas and came to California as did two of his sisters. Gerald and his sister Helen first settled in Fresno; then they moved to Santa Barbara. Gerald became an assistant court reporter for Dewey Carson in Santa Barbara's Superior Court. Helen worked as a nurse.

While in Santa Barbara, Gerald married a second time. His bride, Mary Lou (Marie) Butler, was also a nurse. In January 1942, Gerald enlisted in the Army Air Corps from Kansas. He had three years of college behind him and was currently enrolled at the University of Colorado Law School.

Gerald earned his wings while training at Lubbock Army Flying School. He then went on to Randolph Field near San Antonio, Texas. Nearly all officers of the Army Air Corps underwent rigorous training at Randolph, an architecturally beautiful and outstanding flight school, thusly nicknamed "West Point of the Air." Mary Lou accompanied her husband from training center to training center.

Gerald was assigned to the 13th Command of the Army Air Force as a member of the 5th Heavy Bomb Group. The 13th was assigned the task of staging attacks from the tropical jungles on more than forty remote islands in the South Pacific. The command earned the nickname "The Jungle Force."

As a captain, Gerald flew B-24s and was attached to the 72nd Bomber Squadron. In the February 17, 1944, edition of the Santa Barbara News-Press, Captain Cass was featured as an Air Medal winner after flying twenty-four combat missions in the South Pacific in his beloved plane, the *Mary Lou*.

One of the strategic airfields of the Imperial Japanese Army was located on Biak, a small island in the South Pacific near New Guinea. The Japanese used the airfield as a base for operations in the Pacific Theater.

Captain Cass Gets Oak Leaf Cluster

In addition to a recent report that Captain Gerald M. Cass had been awarded the Air Medal and had participated in 24 combat missions in the South Pacific, an official Army Air Forces dispatch last week announced that he has received the Oak Leaf Cluster "for meritorious achievement while participating in aerial flights on combat, operational missions of a hazardous nature."

His bombing missions have advanced to 27, revealed the report. Captain Cass, whose wife, Mrs. Mary Lou Cass, a nurse now living in Fresno, pilots a heavy Liberator bomber against Jap-held installations in the South Pacific. He has been overseas 10 months. Before leaving the States, the officer attended training schools in San Angelo and Lubbock, Tex.

Cass worked with the Santa Barbara county court reporter, Dewey Carson, at one time and has been in service more than two years. He is flight commander of a group overseas, friends report.

Santa Barbara News Press, March 5, 1944

Santa Barbara's Fallen Aviators of World War II

On May 5, 1944, Captain Cass was to attack this important base. At 11:48 a.m. while flying over Biak, his plane with a crew of eleven was attacked by a Zero (a Japanese fighter plane), and the number two engine was hit. Commander Cass realized his plane could not return to home base, so he attempted a water landing. Witnesses saw men bail from the plane less than five minutes before it hit the water. Two of the crew ultimately survived, nine did not including Commander Cass.

Ironically, while on his last mission, Gerald was promoted from captain to major but he had already taken off and never knew of his promotion. Because of his service, he was awarded the Air Medal. Major Cass also earned four oak clusters and had been recommended for the Distinguished Flying Cross.

His widow received the Air Medal with the Silver Oak Leaf Cluster and an accompanying citation at a ceremony with a full military parade held at Dwight Murphy Field in Santa Barbara. The citation stated in part:

> *"For meritorious achievement, first as a pilot and later as a squadron commander and while participating in sustained combat operation missions in flight which were of a hazardous nature during which enemy opposition was met, or during which an area was traversed where enemy anti-aircraft fire was effective or where enemy fighter patrols were habitually encountered, Captain Gerald M. Cass exhibited great courage and untiring energy, his services reflecting highest credit on the military forces of the United States."*

Perhaps the most touching honor was one bestowed by his own squadron. They named a regulation size baseball diamond Cass Field. The ball field was used by all personnel of the 13th Command of the Army Air Force Flying Skull B-24 Group.

His body was never recovered. Major Cass was memorialized at the American Cemetery at Fort Bonifacio, Manila, Philippines. Besides the Air Medal and Oak Leaf Clusters, his bravery earned him a Purple Heart, and a Santa Barbara Airport street is named for him.

His daughter, Ruth Helen, carried on his memory and became involved with the 31st Bombardment Association, an organization formed to preserve the history of the 31st Bomb Squadron known as the 5th Bomb Group during World War II. She remained a member until her death on March 19, 2008.

Gerald M. Cass Believed Killed In Bomber Crash

Although he is officially listed as "missing in action," Major Gerald M. Cass, considered one of the "most skilled and well liked officers" in his squadron is believed to have been killed in the crash of his bomber after it lost a wing while returning from a combat mission last May 5, it was revealed Tuesday.

Major Cass, who was assistant court-reporter to Dewey Carson at the county courthouse and attended Santa Barbara college, was the pilot of the famous "Mary-Lou" bomber from which he and his crew bombed the Japanese on many missions which won for him the Air Medal and several Oak Leaf Clusters.

According to reports sent in by brother officers and his commander, his airplane was seen to go down and crash in the water. It was the lead plane in a formation that successfully completed its bombing mission. The formation was attacked by enemy fighters and during the running fight that followed, Cass' plane was hit and one motor knocked out.

"Major Cass realized that his airplane could not make it back," the reports disclosed, "so he endeavored to make a water landing. While he was guiding the airplane toward the water, a few members of his crew were seen to parachute out. Major Cass evidently had given the order to jump, because shortly afterward the wing collapsed, and it immediately plunged into the ocean."

Subsequently it was disclosed that two survivors were rescued but they had no news to add.

In a letter to the flier's wife, the commanding officer announced that Cass had been a captain when he went out on that flight but was promoted to the rank of major.

Santa Barbara News Press, July 18, 1944

Sergeant Cecil Palrang Cook, Jr.

Cecil was born July 18, 1917, in Providence, Rhode Island, to immigrant parents, Cecil Cook from England and Margaret Stapleton Cook from Ireland. When Cecil was a young boy, the family came to Santa Barbara where his father worked as a chauffeur for a private family. Cecil had two younger brothers: Bill, born in 1919 and Jim, born in 1933.

Sgt. Cecil P. Cook, Jr.

Cecil attended local schools and graduated from Santa Barbara High School in 1935. He then attended college for two years before enlisting in the Army in 1939. He later joined the Army Air Corps as a private first class and was later promoted to staff sergeant. No record could be found as to what position Sergeant Cook held in the Army Air Corps. He was, however, assigned to the 19th Bomb Group which flew B-17s, the Flying Fortresses of the war.

He was attached to the 93rd Bombardment Squadron when he was taken as a prisoner of war by the Japanese. The War Department listed him as missing in February 1942. A year and a half later in September 1943, his family finally heard from him. Cecil sent a postcard from the prison camp on which he wrote,

> "Everything is OK. Hope to be home soon. Don't worry. Regards to Bill and Jim and everybody."

The date and circumstances of his imprisonment are unknown other than he was incarcerated at Davao Penal Colony in the Philippines. His name, along with other POWs, was secretly noted on a roster buried at the camp on April 15, 1944. The camp was closed June 6 of that year and the prisoners were placed on Japanese carriers to be transported elsewhere.

One of the Japanese carriers was the *Shinyo Maru*, an antiquated freighter pressed into service by the Japanese. On August 14, 1944, US intelligence intercepted a Japanese message indicating that the ship was to unload rice and cement currently in her holds at Zamboanga, Mindanao, and the remaining goods in Manila. Further messages were decoded including one indicating that on September 7, the *Shinyo Maru* was to sail from Manila with 750 troops on board.

The *Shinyo Maru* bore no markings that indicated it was carrying prisoners. The USS *Paddle* was a submarine on its fifth war patrol in the Pacific. While in its patrol area about ten miles north of Sindangan Point, Mindanao, the crew sighted a small convoy which contained the *Shinyo Maru*. The submarine shot at the ship not realizing war prisoners were being transported. It sent two torpedoes into the hold of the ship which prompted the Japanese commander to turn the ship up on to the beach to keep it from sinking.

A machine gun was mounted on the ship's stern with a gunner. The gunner, along with Japanese soldiers in life boats, began to shoot down the prisoners who survived the torpedo hits as they tried to escape from the ship. Six hundred sixty-seven prisoners died while eighty-three others made it to shore, although one died shortly after reaching the beach. Cecil Cook was one of those who did not make it.

Survivors of the slaughter called the *Shinyo Maru* the "Hell Ship;" 750 men had been crammed into the cargo hold for nineteen days before the ship sailed. Eighty-one of the survivors were taken off the Philippine Island and sent to an army hospital in Brisbane, Australia. One American chose to remain on Mindanao to serve as a radio operator under the command of Brigadier General Wendell Fertig. One hundred fifty Japanese lost their lives that day as well.

A memorial dedicated to those who lost their lives on the *Shinyo Maru* on September 7, 1944

Sergeant Cecil Cook's body was never recovered. He was memorialized at the American Cemetery at Fort Bonifacio, Manila, Philippines, and awarded the Purple Heart for his bravery. A Santa Barbara Airport street is named for him.

Lieutenant Earl A. Courville

Earl was a Santa Barbara High School graduate in the Class of 1940. He was born in Worcester, Massachusetts, to Louis and Alice LaFlamme Courville on October 9, 1921, the younger of two sons. His brother, Herbert, did not survive to adulthood.

Alice died when Earl was a boy. His father was a travelling boiler-engineer who was often away and Earl needed a permanent place to live. He stayed for a time with an aunt and uncle on the East Coast until he came to live with his Uncle Frank and Aunt Betty LaFlamme in Santa Barbara. Meanwhile, his father remarried and made his home in Albemarle, North Carolina, where Earl's half sister, Mary Juanita, was born in 1939. Tragically, Louis was killed in an auto accident the following year in South Carolina.

Lt. Earl A. Courville

Earl attended Santa Barbara High School where he joined the ROTC and competed on its fencing team. He was also on the high school yearbook staff serving as the photography assistant. Since his uncle and aunt operated a local photo studio, his responsibilities for the yearbook likely came easily. While in high school Earl was smitten by a pretty girl, Nancy Mecham, who was six years his junior. They had met at the LaFlamme Photography Studio. According to Nancy, because of the age difference, the couple kept their romance quiet.

After high school, Earl wanted to study to become an electrical engineer; instead, the following February, he joined the National Guard as a private first class in the Army's field artillery unit. He trained in Fort Lewis, Washington, before transferring to the Air Force. He was commissioned as a lieutenant in the Air Force in May 1942.

A year later, Lieutenant Courville was flying a P-39 Airacobra out of Hilo, Hawaii, when he was forced to land due to engine failure. Apparently he escaped unhurt. The P-39 was mainly used at the outset of World War II and was the first plane to be designed around a gun. Although its mid-engine placement was innovative, the P-39 design was handicapped by the lack of an efficient turbo-supercharger, limiting it to low altitude work. It was not well liked by American or British pilots, but was successfully used by Soviet airmen.

P-39 Airacobra, an aircraft model flown by Lt. Courville

Lieutenant Courville spent fifteen months of active duty in the South Pacific. He participated in the Battle of Tarawa launched in November 1943 in the mid-Pacific. The intent of this engagement was to gain control of this tiny spit of land where an offensive could be launched to take the strategic Mariana Islands. The battle was won by the Allies but at a heavy price in the loss of lives, and to this day remains controversial as to its strategic importance.

Lieutenant Courville returned to the U.S. and was stationed at Laurinburg-Maxton Army Air Base in North Carolina. There he was assigned to do special experimental work that was likely classified. Ironically, having survived a forced landing a year and a half earlier and the bloody battle of Tarawa, Lieutenant Courville was killed in an automobile accident less than five miles from his home base. Earl died from a fractured skull on October 12, 1944. His body was returned to Santa Barbara and buried in Calvary Cemetery.

**Lt. Earl A. Courville is buried in Calvary Cemetery
Santa Barbara, California**

Lieutenant Robert E. Coverstone

Lt. Robert E. Coverstone

Known as Bob, Robert Coverstone was the oldest of four boys born to Virgil and Ethel Hendricks Coverstone about 1923, probably in Oregon where his three younger brothers, Lanar, Dean, and Dale, were born.

Bob came to live in Santa Barbara with his father after his parents divorced. He graduated from Santa Barbara High School in 1941 and worked for his father's insurance firm until he entered the service.

Bob joined the Army Air Force and began his training in Santa Ana before going on to Blythe. He entered basic training as a bomber pilot at Gardner Field in Taft and took advanced training at Williams Field in Arizona where he earned his wings. Originally he was assigned as a flight instructor at Marana Airfield, also in Arizona, but things changed and he was sent to Salt Lake City and then to Pyote, Texas.

While stationed in Texas, he became engaged to Enid L. King of Oakland. The couple had met while they were living in Salt Lake City. The wedding was planned for June in Oakland but plans were put on hold when Lieutenant Coverstone was sent overseas to England.

Bob was a B-17 pilot with the 422nd Bomber Squadron attached to the 305th Bomber Group in England. B-17 pilots mainly flew in daylight targeting German industrial, civilian, and military sites. The B-17 Flying Fortress was a potent, high-flying, long-ranging bomber capable of unleashing great destruction, able to defend itself, and had the capability to return back to base despite extensive battle damage.

On October 22, 1944, Lieutenant Coverstone was the co-pilot of a B-17 affectionately known as *My Achin' B.* The pilot was Lieutenant Phil Lichty with seven additional crew members on board. Their target was a tank factory northwest of Hanover, Germany. This would be the tenth and final mission of Bob's career. Ironically, if he had lived, he would have been the commanding officer of future missions assigned to him.

According to an eyewitness account, the mission went well but, upon the crew's return to England, the weather turned bad and

The B-17 Flying Fortress, a four-engine heavy bomber, was the model of aircraft flown by Lt. Coverstone

visibility was poor. When the 305th Bomber Group approached Thurleigh Field, other aircraft were in the area and danger appeared imminent. A plane from the 364th Squadron, trying to avoid a collision with another plane, turned away in a steep banking maneuver. That maneuver caused *My Achin' B* to clip a large section of the left wing of the turning plane and both aircraft exploded. Debris from the broken planes as well as the bodies of the men inside were strewn across Thurleigh Airfield. There were no survivors.

Lieutenant Coverstone's father received a letter from the Office of the Chaplain in New York expressing his sympathy. He noted that Bob was given a Christian burial in an American cemetery in England on October 28, 1944, complete with all the honors of a military funeral. In a subsequent letter the chaplain wrote the following:

> *"On the day Robert was killed there were many of us 'sweating the boys in' and I just can't describe how badly we all felt when we knew that the fellows were killed in both of the planes which collided due to bad weather conditions. Robert was in one of the planes which met this ill fate."*

Second Lieutenant Robert E. Coverstone was awarded an Air Medal with two Oak Leaf Clusters for his service. He was honored by Alexis and Marie Witmer of Santa Barbara on the World War II National Memorial Registry of Remembrances established in conjunction with the World War II Memorial in Washington DC. Mr. Witmer had been an aviation navigator who saw service in the Pacific. Perhaps Bob and Alexis had trained together.

Lt. Coverstone seated in an aircraft

LIEUTENANT FRANCIS RICHARD DIBBLEE

Francis Richard Dibblee went by Richard. He was born January 16, 1923, the youngest of four children born to T. Wilson and Anita Orena Dibblee. Both of Richard's parents were descendants of Jose Antonio de la Guerra y Noriega, an early commandante of Santa Barbara.

The Dibblee family lived in a large home on Santa Barbara Street where a cannon from the original presidio graced the front lawn. Richard graduated from Laguna Blanca School and attended Santa Barbara College. He joined the Army Air Corps on October 30, 1942, as a private and received his initial training in Bozeman, Montana, before transferring to Santa Ana in August 1943.

He enrolled in the Hancock College of Aeronautics and then was sent on to Chico to receive additional aviation training in early 1944. Richard received his pilot's training and his silver wings at Fort Sumner, New Mexico. He learned to fly B-24 Liberators. These aircraft were used to haul fuel, transport VIPs, patrol for submarines, and drop supplies by parachute. Until the B-29, the B-24 was the most modern aircraft with the latest equipment. It also gradually replaced the B-17 in the heavy bomber role, largely because of the B-24's greater range.

Courtesy of Dibblee Hoyt
Lieutenant Francis. R. Dibblee

Richard was commissioned a second lieutenant and sent to the Pacific as a co-pilot assigned to the 98th Bombardment Squadron, part of the 11th Bombardment Group. The 11th was

Courtesy of Dibblee Hoyt
A B-24 Liberator, similar to the plane flown by Lt. Dibblee and his crew

based at Harmon Field on the island of Guam. On May 8, 1945, a B-24J took off from Harmon Field at 9:00 a.m. local time with Lieutenant John K. Lowe at the controls and Second Lieutenant Dibblee as his co-pilot. There were nine other crew members on board this aircraft nicknamed *The Temptation*. Eleven other planes took off at the same time with the purpose of extricating the enemy from Marcus Island, a spit of isolated land in the northwestern part of the Pacific Ocean. When the planes approached their target, they were met by enemy fire over the island. *The Temptation* was hit just prior to making its bomb run, forcing the pilot to ditch into the ocean. The crew was approximately seventy-five miles from the nearest base at Saipan, China.

All of the crew members of the B-24J were killed except the navigator, Harold L. Vigue, and the gunner, Corporal Raymond De Roo. A few days later, Mr. and Mrs. Dibblee received the sad news via telegram that Richard had died. Ironically, they had just received a letter written by their son dated May 6. It had been sent from the Marianas where he had arrived a few days earlier from Honolulu. In it he described the food they had brought from Hawaii, his crew members, and his new living quarters. Raised a Catholic, he ended his letter by saying he planned to go to Communion on Mother's Day.

Lt. Francis Dibblee pictured with his crew

Lieutenant Dibblee's body was never recovered, and his name is inscribed on the Tablets of the Missing at the National Memorial Cemetery of the Pacific, Honolulu, Hawaii.

He was awarded the Air Medal and Purple Heart posthumously. Harold Vigue, the navigator on the ill-fated flight, honored his friend Richard Dibblee on the National World War II Memorial Registry of Remembrances established in conjunction with the World War II Memorial in Washington DC. The final irony to Lieutenant Dibblee's story was the return of Marcus Island to the Japanese after the war.

Santa Barbara News Press, **June 6, 1945**

Lieutenant John Louis Donaldson

John was known as Jack to family and friends. He was born August 19, 1922, in Waltham, Massachusetts, to William and Marion Harding Donaldson. His parents were Canadian born and moved to Massachusetts in 1917. William began to experience health problems and it was thought perhaps moving to a milder climate would benefit him. In 1935, Santa Barbara became their new home.

Jack attended Santa Barbara High School where he played left tackle for the football team. He graduated in 1940, and briefly attended Santa Barbara State College. He joined the Army Air Force in December 1940 because he wanted to learn to fly. He trained at Fort Sumner, New Mexico, and earned his glider pilot's wings. A highlight for Jack was taking General Jimmy Doolittle on the General's first glider ride.

Jack began his formal pilot's training at Hawthorne Field in North Carolina. He was commissioned a second lieutenant at his graduation ceremony at Turner Field in Georgia. He was a flight instructor there before going on to Chicago to learn to fly the B-17, known as the Flying Fortress. The B-17 was primarily used in daylight bombing missions against German industrial, civilian, and military targets; crews of the four-engine heavy bomber were often based in England.

Lieutenant John L. Donaldson

Lieutenant Donaldson was indeed sent to England in 1944 to join the 100th Bomber Group as a pilot of the 350th Squadron. He had been in the service for four years and this was his first overseas assignment. He arrived in England on June 15.

Twelve days later, Lieutenant Donaldson was flying *Boss Lady* with a crew of nine on a practice mission when the aircraft crashed into the sea carrying its crew to the bottom. The plane was last seen in the air about five miles north of Yarmouth with adequate visibility. The cause of the accident remains unknown to this day and no bodies were recovered. *Boss Lady* and her crew never saw combat.

Lt. John Donaldson, his mother, Marion, and brother, George

Lieutenant Jack Donaldson was remembered by his brother, Captain George Donaldson, on the National World War II Memorial Registry of Remembrances established in conjunction with the World War II Memorial dedicated in Washington DC in 2004. He is also remembered on the World War II Memorial at Santa Barbara High School. A street at the Santa Barbara Airport bears John Donaldson's name.

**The crew of the *Boss Lady*.
Lt. Donaldson front row, on the left**

Lieutenant Rex Albert Eckles

According to Howard Eckles, his brother Rex was a handsome young man almost 6'1" and destined to be a pilot. Rex was born May 19, 1919, in Porterville, California, to Berthal (Bert) and Mattie Smith Eckles. Bert worked for Western Weld Drilling Company in the San Joaquin Valley before he transferred to Santa Barbara.

Rex attended Santa Barbara High School and graduated in 1937. While in high school, he was a commissioned officer in ROTC and in the Scholarship Society. After high school, he enrolled in the University Farm School at Davis (now UC Davis) to study agriculture. After a year, he transferred to Santa Barbara College where he took general studies courses.

Rex had a real love for flying and in October 1941, he enlisted as an aviation cadet in the Army Air Force. His training began at a flight school near Tulare, and he completed his flight instruction at Mather Airbase near Sacramento in May 1942. It was there Rex received his wings. Two days before Rex shipped out, he married Mary Jane Boggs, a fellow student at Santa Barbara College.

Lt. Rex A. Eckles

In 1942, Lieutenant Eckles was assigned to the 431st Bombardment Squadron as part of the 11th Bombardment Group in Hawaii. He was flying a B-17E Flying Fortress called *Tokyo Taxi* with a crew of nine. Only five B-17 groups were operating in the South Pacific at this time, with other groups converting to aircraft other than the B-17.

Courtesy of Gray Geese Calling
The *Tokyo Taxi*, of which Lt. Eckles was the pilot, being serviced in 1942

In November 1942, the plane and crew were sent to Carney Field on Guadalcanal as part of the 5th Bombardment Group and assigned to the 23rd Bombardment Squadron. The following July 4, Lieutenant General Millard F. Harmon, Commanding U.S. Army Forces in the South Pacific area, handed out awards to 150 men who had represented gallantry in land, sea, and air fighting. Lieutenant Eckles was one of six men from Santa Barbara to receive recognition. He was awarded the Air Medal. Late on July 18, 1943, Rex, his eight crew members, and one other passenger took off in their B-17 for a night bombing mission against the Japanese. Their target was Kahili Airfield on the island of Bougainville. Lieutenant Eckles was the pilot of the lead plane and easily a target when caught in enemy searchlights on the ground.

Santa Barbara's Fallen Aviators of World War II

The plane was last seen at 2:30 a.m. eight to ten miles north of Kahili Airfield. It had been armed with four 30-caliber machine guns in the nose and 50-caliber machine guns in other positions.

Lieutenant Eckles's best friend and roommate Anthony Dean Lucas was the pilot of *Li'l Nell* flying directly behind *Tokyo Taxi*. Captain Lucas watched as his friend's plane exploded under a barrage of bombs. He described the action:

> "Nine ships of our squadron took off around midnight to bomb Kahili Airfield. All my bombs hit on target from 14,000 feet. While on the beginning of my bombing run I saw one of my best friends go down in flames. Shot down by Jap night fighters. He was Lt., soon to be Capt. Eckles, of Santa Barbara. We had been together for the past year in the 23rd. We were both (flight school class) 42E men. His was a real crew, with some swell men, co-pilot, Lt. Jones; a classmate of my co-pilot, Bomb. Lt. Knop, Nav. Lt. Fox, Enj., Sgt. Kelly, Ass. Enj. Sgt. Greene, Radio Sgt. Davis, Hill and a couple of other men."

After giving his statement, he asked if one day he could take his friend's personal belongings home to Rex's parents and wife in Santa Barbara.

Two aircraft unsuccessfully searched for the downed B-17 later that morning. Only a CO_2 bottle was spotted. The crew was officially listed as Missing in Action before finally being declared dead on January 11, 1946.

Captain Lucas named his son Rex in honor of his fallen friend. Posthumously, Lieutenant Eckles was awarded the Air Medal and Purple Heart. He is memorialized on the Tablets of the Missing at the American Cemetery in Manila, Philippines, along with six of his crew members. The others are listed on the Tablets of the Missing at the National Memorial Cemetery of the Pacific, Honolulu, Hawaii. Lieutenant Eckles is remembered on the World War II Memorial at Santa Barbara High School, and a street at the Santa Barbara Airport is named for him.

Flight crew of the *Tokyo Taxi*. Lt. Rex Eckles is in bottom row, first on left

Sixty-six years later, Captain Lucas's two children, Gwendolyn and Rex, visited Guadalcanal. They stood on the remnants of the old airfield now choked by jungle but at one time a temporary home to their father and his best friend. There they dug up pieces of the runway to give to Howard Eckles, Rex's brother. After searching over the years for members of the Eckles's family, Gwendolyn and Rex finally had the chance to meet the lieutenant's brother and share their father's memory of his best friend.

LIEUTENANT NORMAN SELWYN FIRESTONE

Norman was born in Butte, Montana, about 1921, the older of two sons born to Irving and Evelyn Cohen Firestone. The family relocated to Santa Barbara where his younger brother was born in 1925. Irving and Evelyn owned a women's clothing store on State Street for many years. Norman and his brother, Gerald, attended Santa Barbara High School; Norman graduated in 1938. While in high school, Norman was the yearbook business manager, a member of the varsity fencing team, and a first lieutenant in the ROTC. He was a good student, a member of the Scholarship Society, and a Seal Bearer. Following high school, Norman attended the University of California, Berkeley as a pre-med student before graduating in May 1942.

Norman Firestone as a Santa Barbara High School ROTC cadet, 1938

In June, he was called to active duty as a reserve infantry officer with the rank of lieutenant. In August, he was plucked from infantry training and sent for pre-flight training in Santa Ana, then onto Yuma, Arizona, and Bartow, Florida, for further flight instruction.

Lieutenant Firestone was assigned to the 74th Fighter Squadron, an Air Force unit of the 23rd Fighter Group. During the war, the 74th was one of the original squadrons in the 23rd to see combat action in the Far East. The Fighter Group flew P-40 Warhawk planes and later P-51 Mustangs to cover a large operational area which extended beyond China into Burma, Vietnam, and Taiwan. Lieutenant Firestone was a P-51 pilot. The P-51 Mustang was a long-range single-crew member fighter aircraft. It was mainly used in Europe to escort bombers but did see limited service against the Japanese in the Pacific War. It was fast, well-made, and highly durable.

The missions for the 23rd Fighter Group included counter air campaigns, strafing and bombing of Japanese forces and installations, escorting bombers, flying reconnaissance missions, and intercepting Japanese bombers.

The P-51 Mustang, the type of aircraft flown by Lt. Firestone

Lieutenant Firestone was attached to the Luliang Airfield in Far Eastern China when he took off on the morning of November 12, 1944. Visibility was fairly good when his plane was strafed near Hengyang Airfield in southeastern China. According to the Missing Air Crew Report (MACR), there were no witnesses as to what happened to the plane or the pilot so he was initially listed as Missing in Action. Apparently his body was recovered sometime later as Norman was buried in the Santa Barbara Cemetery on October 28, 1947.

Gerald Firestone also served in the Army as a crew member on a B-17 Flying Fortress. He came home safely from the war, married, and had two children. In the late 1960s, he was elected mayor of Santa Barbara. He passed away in 1980.

Lieutenant Norman Firestone is honored on the Santa Barbara High School World War II Memorial. A street at the Santa Barbara Airport also bears his name.

Lt. Norman Firestone, Mustang Pilot, Missing In China

First Lieutenant Norman S. Firestone, Mustang fighter pilot stationed in China and a graduate of Santa Barbara High school, is missing in action. He is 24 years old.

A telegram announcing the news was delivered to his parents, Mr. and Mrs. Irving Firestone, 11 West Junipero street, Sunday at noon. He has been missing since Nov. 12.

The officer has been overseas since Sept. 2. His parents had heard from him three times since he left the States and in his last letter, dated Nov. 2 and delivered here Nov. 12, he revealed that he was "in a wonderful squadron" and expected to see action soon.

Lieutenant Firestone graduated from the University of California at Berkeley as a pre-medical student. He took his training at Barstow, Fla., and had been in uniform for 30 months. He has one brother, Private Gerald S. Firestone, now taking training at the aerial gunnery school in Las Vegas, Nev.

Santa Barbara News Press, December 11, 1944

Lieutenant Norman Selwyn Firestone is buried in Santa Barbara Cemetery, Santa Barbara, California

LIEUTENANT JAMES LAURENCE FOWLER

James (known as Jim) and his two sisters were born in Santa Barbara to Laurence and Margaret MacDonald Fowler. The children were educated in local schools and Jim attended Santa Barbara High School where he played the trumpet and earned his captain's stripes in ROTC. He graduated in 1939 and attended Pomona College for a time before returning to Santa Barbara to attend the local state college.

Lt. James L. Fowler

In 1942, while a college student, Jim enlisted in the Navy as an aviation cadet with three other fellow students. Their initial training was at St. Mary's College in Moraga (east of Oakland, California). Jim received further training and graduated from the Naval Air Training Center at Corpus Christi, Texas, and was commissioned a second lieutenant in the Marine Corps Reserves.

In October 1943, Jim married Frances (Nan) Bacon Colt at All-Saints-By-The-Sea Episcopal Church in Montecito. It had all the trappings of a military-style wedding with the matron of honor and bridesmaids wearing the marine colors of blue and yellow. The groom, his best man, and the ushers wore Marine full-dress blues.

At the time of his marriage, Lieutenant Fowler was living at the Marine Corps Air Station, Santa Barbara and undergoing training as a torpedo bombing pilot. Before he shipped out, he reported to San Diego and then was sent to the South Pacific in December. He saw heavy action almost immediately, and in March 1944, his parents received a telegram stating their son had been missing since February 14.

Lieutenant Fowler was flying a TBF-1 Avenger, a torpedo bomber developed initially for the United States Navy and Marine Corps. It entered US service in 1942, and first saw action during the Battle of Midway. There were three crew members on board: pilot, turret gunner, and radioman/bombardier/ventral gunner. One 30-caliber machine gun was mounted in the nose, a 50-caliber gun was mounted right next to the turret gunner's head and a single 30-caliber hand-fired machine gun was mounted under the tail and used to defend against enemy aircraft attacking from below and to the rear. It also had a large bomb bay allowing a torpedo or bomb to be stored. The aircraft was rugged and stable, and pilots said it flew like a truck. It also had excellent radio facilities.

TBF-1 Avenger, a torpedo bomber shown here dropping a torpedo, was the type of aircraft flown by Lt. James Fowler

On the night of February 14, 1944, Lieutenant Fowler and his two crewmen took off from Torokina Airfield (on the island of Bougainville) with several other aircraft. The mission was to drop aerial mines into Simpson Harbor from 800 feet at a slow speed. The harbor was a Japanese stronghold on the eastern end of the island of New Britain, Papua New Guinea. A total of six Avengers went down in this mission including Fowler's plane.

The crew was declared dead the following day though the family was not informed of this status until much later. In December, Nan, the aviator's wife, received a letter from Colonel R. H. Jeschke of the United States Marine Corps stating that her husband had been awarded the Distinguished Flying Cross. He further wrote that First Lieutenant James L. Fowler was still in the records as Missing in Action and the decoration with its accompanying citation would be held in his office in case the lieutenant should be available for presentation of the award at some later time. With his letter he sent an official copy of the citation:

Santa Barbara News Press, March 16, 1944

> *"Participating in an attack upon enemy shipping Simpson Harbor, Rabaul, Jan. 31, First Lieutenant J.L. Fowler scored a direct hit upon a large cargo vessel in face of determined Japanese fire, leaving her in a sinking condition.*
>
> *"During a night aerial mine laying mission in the same harbor on Feb. 14, he skillfully and courageously completed a long, level flight at slow air speed and precariously low altitude directly over a solid concentration of heavy automatic anti-aircraft weapons and searchlights. Spotted by numerous Japanese searchlights before reaching his objective and forced to maneuver his plane through intense and accurate fire from both shore and ship batteries, he remained steadfast to his course and despite severe damage to his plane, released his mine in its assigned position.*
>
> *"First Lieutenant J.L. Fowler's superb airmanship and unswerving devotion to duty in the face of grave peril throughout his combat missions were in keeping with the highest traditions of the U. S. Naval Service."*

Lieutenant Fowler's status was finally changed to Killed in Action and he is remembered on the Fort William McKinley Monument in Manila, Philippines. He was awarded the Purple Heart for his bravery. On September 6, 1945, the Japanese surrendered all remaining Japanese forces in New Guinea, New Britain, and the Solomon Islands. The ceremony took place on the aircraft carrier HMS *Glory*.

Lieutenant Fowler's service to his country is remembered on several local memorials. He is honored on the World War II Memorial at Santa Barbara High School. The street which fronts the Santa Barbara Airport terminal bears James Fowler's name.

LIEUTENANT AUGUSTUS MONROE GRIGGS, JR.

Lt. Augustus M. Griggs

Augustus and his only sibling, Bernice, were the first members of their family to be born in California. Augustus was born December 22, 1921, in Santa Barbara to Augustus Senior and Sarah Dodsworth Griggs.

He attended local schools including Santa Barbara High School where he played football. He did not graduate but enlisted in the artillery branch of the National Guard on February 3, 1941. That same year he married Barbara Harshbarger.

Augustus and Barbara became parents when daughter Sue Ann was born in September 1942 in Santa Barbara. He had ended his service with the National Guard and had joined the Army Air Force as an air cadet. He received his basic training at the Santa Ana Army Air Base (SAAAB) which had opened earlier in the year. After nine weeks of training, the men were tested to determine if they were to be pilots, bombardiers, navigators, or mechanics. Out of more than 23,000 soldiers graduating from SAAAB, Augustus was one of the select few chosen for pilot training.

He was transferred to Ryan-Hemet Airfield in Riverside County to attend the Ryan School of Aeronautics in spring 1943. The school was contracted by the Army Air Force to give elementary and advanced flight training to Army pilots. Augustus earned his wings when he graduated from Williams Field in Arizona and also received his commission as a second lieutenant in the Army Air Forces.

Following his graduation, he was assigned to Muroc Airfield in California where he flew P-38 pursuit ships. When his plane crashed on August 14, 1943, he was flying an RP-38IE, a re-designated P-38 that was restricted from use in combat because of its age. He was slated to become a flight instructor at the Santa Ana Airfield where he trained. He was killed near Granite Rock in Riverside County. Lieutenant Griggs had taken off early in the morning and was flying at a low altitude over Camp Granite when his left propeller touched the ground. The engine stalled and he attempted to gain altitude using the right engine. After climbing approximately 150 feet, both engines quit, the plane went into a spin, and then crashed. Pilot Griggs did not survive.

He never saw combat but died serving his country stateside. Lieutenant Griggs is buried in the Santa Barbara Cemetery; a Santa Barbara Airport street is named for him.

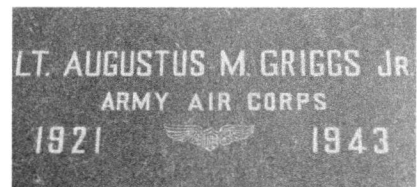

Like so many young men in World War II, John Donaldson and Augustus Griggs were classmates in high school, playing varsity football together. Each enlisted in the United States Army Air Force, both became pilots, and both, ultimately, gave their lives in defense of their country.

Augustus Griggs, pictured above on the right, with John Donaldson, on the left, in their varsity football photograph at Santa Barbara High School in 1940.

Captain William Miller Harshbarger

Known as Bill, William M. Harshbarger was born on March 16, 1917, in the small town of St. Anthony, Idaho, to Dr. Miller and Grace Campbell Harshbarger. When Bill was just nine years old, his father developed a fatal infection and died. His grieving widow moved to Santa Barbara with her parents, her sister, and her two young children to start a new life.

Bill's mother married a rancher and Bill took to ranch life, learning to ride horses and to compete in rodeo events. He attended Santa Barbara High School and graduated in 1936. He then enrolled at the University of California, College of Agriculture at Davis to study agriculture. He, too, wanted to be a rancher.

After war was declared but before the United States entered the conflict, Bill and a group of his childhood friends enlisted in the Army. They wanted to serve their country. Bill knew he wanted to be an aviator, but he was in a precarious position because of a bad knee, the result of many injuries riding and working with horses. He was determined not to let his friends or his country down and successfully passed the physical exam, though not an easy task. He nearly passed out when the doctor "hammered" his bad knee.

Captain William M. Harshbarger

The B-24 Liberator, an American heavy bomber, similar to the one flown by Captain William Harshbarger

Bill entered the military as an Air Corps cadet on March 18, 1941, and received his pilot's training at March Air Field in Riverside County. Bill earned his wings at Luke Field, Arizona, and then was stationed at Hickam Field in Hawaii when the Japanese bombed Pearl Harbor on December 7, 1941.

He saw action at Midway as a member of the famous 26th Bombardment Squadron which also took an active role in the Battle of the Solomons. Lieutenant Harshbarger flew the B-24 Liberator, a heavy bomber with a 1200-mile range that could carry a bomb load weighing as much as 5500 pounds. The B-24 was also used to haul fuel, transport VIPs, patrol for submarines, and drop supplies by parachute. It also flew reconnaissance and assessed weather conditions. In the early part of the war, it was the only heavy American bomber covering the seas from Alaska to India.

After taking part in fifty-four missions and serving for twenty months in the Pacific, Lieutenant Harshbarger returned home in March 1943 and married a local girl, Sally Townsend. He wore his full military dress uniform in the ceremony performed at All-Saints-By-The-Sea Episcopal Church in Montecito. In character with his free outdoors spirit, he immediately took off his tie ("to loosen up at the reception") after being photographed emerging from the church with his bride!

Lieutenant Harshbarger, now home safely and with a new bride, was assigned to the Salinas Air Field as a flight instructor before transferring to Walla Walla, Washington.

There, on June 10, 1944, he was awarded the Distinguished Flying Cross and the Air Medal during a formal retreat parade. He was promoted to captain and was teaching young aviators to fly the B-24 Liberator to finish out the war.

> Captain Harshbarger Dies In Washington Crash

Headline from *Santa Barbara News Press* article, July 20, 1944

Ironically, just weeks later, Captain Harshbarger and his crew of eleven were killed when their Liberator aircraft crashed near Walla Walla on July 19. On the day he died, as he had every day since his adolescence, he was wearing the belt with the silver buckle one of the ranch workers had once made for him. His body was returned to Santa Barbara where funeral services were held. Pallbearers included several members of the military.

Bill and Sally had no children. In 1949, she married David Knowles of Montecito. They had three children, one of whom she named after her beloved Bill. Sally and David lived and raised their children on a ranch in Coleville in eastern California – a life similar to the one Bill and Sally had planned before his death. Sally died there at the age of eighty-one.

LIEUTENANT CYRIL OWEN HARTLEY

Cyril was born August 12, 1921, in Santa Barbara to Cyril and Daisy Ripken Hartley. The elder Cyril was at one time the Ford dealer in Carpinteria where the family lived until their son was a junior in high school. The family moved to Santa Barbara and Cyril graduated in 1939 from Santa Barbara High. The high school yearbook described Cyril as a "tall, rather quiet fellow, who came to Santa Barbara in his junior year from Carpinteria." Cyril had been an active member of the Social Committee and ROTC while in high school.

Lt. Cyril O. Hartley

He enrolled at Santa Barbara State College then transferred to the College of the Pacific as a mathematics major. Cyril enlisted in the Army in August 1940 while still in college. He did not begin military training for another year, but when the United States was attacked at Pearl Harbor, Cyril was actively serving in the Army. He was initially assigned to Mather Field in Sacramento with the rank of sergeant.

He was reassigned very quickly as an Air Corps cadet and took his training at Kelly Field in Texas. Less than a month later, he advanced to the rank of cadet flight sergeant. Out of the initial class of 200, Cyril was one of only seventy-five to complete the basic flight training course by March 1942.

His next assignment for more advanced training was at Randolph Field near San Antonio, Texas. He completed his training back at Kelly Field later that year where he earned his wings as a bomber pilot and was promoted to lieutenant.

Lieutenant Hartley never saw action overseas. He trained others to fly using the BT-13A Valiant. It was the most widely-used American training aircraft of World War II. The aircraft had a continuous canopy with its crew of two sitting in tandem behind dual controls. It was also equipped with blind flying instruments to teach new pilots the basics of flying at night or in foul weather. When production ceased in 1944, 11,535 Valiants had been produced. They were retired at the end of the war.

The BT-13A Valiant aircraft, which Lt. Hartley used in training cadets to fly

Santa Barbara's Fallen Aviators of World War II

Sadly, on May 15, 1943, the BT-13 Lieutenant Hartley and his cadet were flying crashed three-quarters of a mile from Perrin Field in Sherman, Texas. Apparently while attempting to correct his student's flying error, Lieutenant Hartley took control of the aircraft so abruptly, the plane stalled. He was unable to regain altitude and the aircraft crashed and burned killing both men. The Lieutenant's cremated remains were returned to Santa Barbara and buried in the Santa Barbara Cemetery.

Cyril's sacrifice for his country is noted on the Elings Park County Veterans Terrace of Remembrance, the Carpinteria High School Memorial, and the Santa Barbara High School Memorial to alumni who gave their lives in defense of their country. Lieutenant Hartley was also honored with a street bearing his name at the Santa Barbara Airport.

Cyril's father died three years later in Santa Barbara just three weeks shy of his fifty-fifth birthday. Daisy died at age eighty-eight; they are buried on either side of their only child who died doing what he loved – flying.

Santa Barbaran Killed in Crash

Texas Accidents Take Seven Lives

Lieut. Cyril Owen Hartley, Jr., 21, of Santa Barbara and Sherman, Tex., was killed Saturday when his Army training plane crashed and burned near Perrin field, Dennison, Tex., according to press dispatches and word received by his parents here.

Hartley was a flying instructor and Aviation Cadet Leon E. Daubert, 22, of Lebanon, Pa., also was killed in the same crash, post authorities reported.

Young Hartley had married a Texas girl since leaving Santa Barbara and they made their home in Sherman, Tex.

He is the son of Mr. and Mrs. Cyril O. Hartley of 1601 San Pascual street and had graduated from Santa Barbara High school. Also he had attended Santa Barbara State college for a year and a half before enlisting.

Young Hartley's widow will arrive here Tuesday night with his remains for funeral services and burial in Santa Barbara.

Santa Barbara News Press,
May 16, 1943

Private John William Hays

John was the oldest son born to William Washington "Wash" and Florence Peterson Hays on November 9, 1912, almost a year after the couple married. He was the second baby born in the original St. John's Hospital in Oxnard, at the corner of F and Fifth.

Two more sons were born to Wash and Florence before they divorced. The boys grew up in the Conejo Valley and attended Oxnard High School. John quit school before graduating, married fellow classmate Ruth Peck, and moved to Ogden, Utah, where their first son Kenneth "Keni" was born. The young family returned to California and moved to Santa Barbara. John went to work for H & H Roofing owned by his wife's uncle, Emmett Hewston. John became the company foreman.

Private John William Hays

John and Ruth were going through some rough times and John decided to join the military. He was ineligible for the draft but he could, at age thirty-two, enlist. He became an Army paratrooper.

John joined the 503rd Parachute Infantry Regiment which was formed in February 1942. He trained with his unit at Fort Benning, Georgia. Unlike many other airborne units who were deployed in the European Theater, the 503rd was the first airborne regiment to fight in the Pacific and as an independent unit.

The 503rd was involved in several Pacific operations particularly during battles in Dutch New Guinea and the Philippines. During the Battle of Mindoro, the 503rd was subjected to intense air and naval actions. The success of the Mindoro operation enabled the US Army Air Force to construct and operate air strips and forward air bases to support later landings.

John Hays playing the banjo earlier in his life

On February 16, 1945, the 503rd jumped on Fortress Corregidor to liberate that island from occupying Japanese forces. The assault was the most intense combat action engaged in by the 503rd. Braving intense fire, the paratroopers rushed forward and overcame the heavy blockhouse defenses, then dropped explosives killing hidden Japanese gunners. For its successful capture of Corregidor, the unit was awarded a Presidential Unit Citation and received its nickname, "The Rock Regiment."

During a subsequent intense battle in the Philippine Theater on April 21, 1945, John parachuted to the ground safely but was later captured by the enemy and shot. His body was buried with many other American soldiers in a long trench on one of the Philippine Islands. His mother was notified by telegram that John had died.

After the war was over, the bodies were exhumed and their remains labeled. The army sent one set of papers to John's wife along with a grave number on it while another set was sent to John's mother indicating a different grave number. A body was then flown back to the States and buried in a plot in the Santa Paula Cemetery. Due to the conflicting paperwork, no one knows if the body buried as John W. Hays is actually his but the family likes to think so.

As his wife, Ruth was initially offered the flag that draped John's casket but she declined, and suggested instead giving it to Florence, his mother. Florence eventually gave it to John's younger son, Jerry. When Jerry died, it passed to his son John, the aviator's grandson and namesake.

**Gravemarker for Private John William Hays,
Santa Paula Cemetery, Santa Paula, California**

LIEUTENANT FRANCIS FREDERICK HEBEL

Lt. Francis Frederick Hebel

Francis Frederick Hebel, known as Fritz, was the last of eight children born to Frank and Wilhelmina (Minnie) Loga Hebel, seven of whom survived to adulthood. Fritz was born in Janesville, Wisconsin, on January 25, 1912.

After the First World War was over, the family moved to Carpinteria. They had visited the beach community in years past and had made friends with the Sawyers from Wisconsin who also owned a dairy and a fruit orchard in the Carpinteria Valley. Ironically, their son Clarence, like Fritz, also became an aviator and lost his life during World War II.

Fritz attended local schools and graduated from Carpinteria High School in 1929. Fritz had been an active student. In his senior year, he was Student Body Vice-President and a member of the Varsity Club, playing football and basketball.

After high school, Fritz went on to Cal Tech in Pasadena and graduated in 1934. He enlisted in the Navy in 1936 in its nascent aviation cadet program. He trained in Pensacola, Florida, and earned his wings in 1937. He became a flight instructor at the Grosse Isle, Michigan, Naval Reserve Air Base. In March 1941, he was commissioned a lieutenant (j.g.) and was sent off to Hawaii where he was assigned to Fighting Squadron Six in the Pacific Fleet based in Pearl Harbor. His job was to teach trainees how to land their planes on aircraft carriers.

F4F Wildcats, the aircraft flown by Lt. Hebel

The Fighting Six was attached to the aircraft carrier *Enterprise* when the Japanese struck Pearl Harbor on December 7, 1941. The ship was not docked in the harbor at the time of the attack but a series of unfortunate circumstances caused Lieutenant Hebel to be the first war casualty from Santa Barbara County. The *Enterprise* crew first learned of the attack just after 8:00 a.m. The first four planes to take off from the carrier were led by Lieutenant Hebel. Others followed as the ship's captain determined where to search for enemy aircraft. As dusk settled in, Hebel's fliers happened to separate from the rest of the group.

Courtesy of CV6.org

The USS Enterprise, to which Lt. Francis F. Hebel was attached at the time Pearl Harbor was attacked, December 7, 1941

John B. Lundstrom describes what happened in his account *The First Team: Pacific Naval Air Combat from Pearl Harbor to Midway* (September 2005):

> *"He [Hebel] skillfully used his Zed Baker radio homing receiver to take the escort directly back to the task force. Somewhat surprised to discover some of the strike planes overhead, Halsey [commander of carrier operations] at about 1950 directed Hebel to fly north to Oahu and to land there. The fighters dutifully headed off into the night, bound for a blacked-out and apprehensive destination."*

Mr. Lundstrom went on to describe Lt. Hebel's mission:

> *"Fritz Hebel at the head of VF-6's escort fighter spotted ahead of him in the blackness an island dotted with fires. Thinking it was Kauai with its burning canefields, he turned east and ended up over Molokai before he realized his error. The fires actually blazed on Oahu as reminders of the savage enemy attack. Checking with his pilots to make certain they had sufficient fuel, Hebel led the six Grummans across the channel west to Makapuu Point on Oahu. From there they followed the coastline south and west over Diamond Head and Waikiki toward the Pearl Harbor Channel entrance south of the harbor proper. Around 2110, Hebel noticed runway lights illuminating the Army's*

Hickam Field just east of the harbor channel….Hebel took the flight north past Hickam.

"The six F4Fs had descended to about 500 feet and turned on their red and green running lights. They started around the Army field, but during the circuit north Hebel noticed the floodlights at Ford Island further north….The six F4Fs cruised at 500 feet with running lights prominent during the short hop over to Ford Island. They offered every appearance of executing a routine night landing. Automatically Hebel banked to the right to circle Ford Island counterclockwise…the turn swept the six F4Fs opposite the Ford Island control tower and over Drydock Channel and Battleship Row, scenes of some of the worst destruction of the raid.

"On board the battered ships, distraught gunners fully believed that the enemy had returned….Captain James M. Shoemaker, in charge of NAS Pearl Harbor, later remarked: 'Somebody let fly, and I never saw so many bullets in the air – all tracer bullets at night.' He thought Hebel's fighters had become the target of 'every gun in the Pearl Harbor area, near as I could tell.' Without warning, the VF-6 pilots became the focus of intense antiaircraft fire. Hebel in shock radioed, 'My God, what's happened!'"

The first plane shot down belonged to Ens. Herbert H. Menges, Lt. Hebel's wingman. Then the last plane in the formation was shot down and its pilot later died. The four remaining F4Fs scattered, each pilot for his own life. Lundstrom tells what happened next:

"Fritz Hebel swung northward, seeking a haven at the Army's Wheeler Field…. Antiaircraft batteries north of there forced Hebel to sheer off. He gunned his engine to pull away from the shooting, but the Pratt & Whitney, perhaps damaged, sputtered and died.

"Hebel had to find someplace to set her down quickly. In the blackness, he had to settle for a canefield north of Aeia. Skidding along the broken, stubbled ground, the F4F cartwheeled, tore in two, and piled into a small gully. Part of the wreckage burst into flames. Onlookers pulled the unconscious pilot from the shattered cockpit and took him to the Army hospital at Schofield Barracks. Having suffered a severe skull fracture, Hebel died the next day."

On the first day of war, the Fighting Six saw no Japanese, yet sustained terrible

Wheeler Field was a primary target in the attack on Pearl Harbor, December 7, 1941

losses: three pilots killed and four F4F-3As destroyed and one badly damaged. Fritz Hebel's family was not notified of his death until word was received by telegram on December 18, and they would not learn the circumstances of his fatality until the end of the war.

Lieutenant Hebel was buried at the National Memorial Cemetery of the Pacific in Honolulu, Hawaii, quite near the grave of noted war correspondent Ernie Pyle.

The memory of Fritz has been honored several ways. The Carpinteria High School stadium was dedicated on November 11, 2009, in memory of military men from the area who lost their lives in various wars with Francis Frederick Hebel among those honored. In 1946, the Carpinteria Valley Post of the Veterans of Foreign Wars was named for Francis Frederick Hebel until it disbanded in 2009.

Santa Barbara News Press,
December 20, 1941

Lieutenant Hebel was buried at the
National Memorial Cemetery of the Pacific,
Honolulu, Hawaii

Lieutenant Robert Louis Keister

Very little is known about Robert Keister except he was born November 23, 1917, in Ohio to Thaddeus L. and Lanorah Hands Keister. His parents had married earlier that same year in Marion County, Indiana. They later divorced when Robert was still a child. His mother remarried and, with her son, moved to Milwaukee where her husband worked in a knitting factory. Robert's father remained in Ohio and also married again.

Robert joined the United States Marine Corps from the state of Indiana when he was of age, and by mid-1937 he had reported to the Marine Base in San Diego. He re-enlisted in October 1940 as a corporal and in November of that year, Robert married Louise E. Irwin, an Illinois native.

He began flight training in November 1941 and won his pilot wings in May 1942. Part of his training occurred at the Marine Corps Air Station in Santa Barbara while he and Louise lived in Santa Barbara. He was next assigned to Fighting Squadron Two of the 2nd Marine Aircraft Group where he achieved the rank of first lieutenant.

Lieutenant Keister was sent overseas in February 1943. By then he had been in the Marine Corps for nearly six years and was a Corsair fighter pilot. The Corsair quickly became the most capable carrier-based fighter-bomber of World War II. It was considerably faster than the Hellcat and only slightly slower than the P-47 Thunderbolt and was the favorite of the US Marine Corps. Corsairs were flown by the famous "Black Sheep" Squadron led by Marine Major "Pappy" Boyington.

Lieutenant Keister had his own moment of personal victory while flying with three other Marine Corps fighter pilots on a mission over the Solomon Islands. Their target was Kara Field, one of the Solomon airfields held by the Japanese. When the four pilots took off from an undisclosed location, a storm was closing fast over their airfield. As they flew over the Shortland Islands, the pilots found themselves faced with an almost impassable storm front.

While desperately looking for an opening in the leaded skies, the fliers finally found one and climbed higher reaching nearly 4000 feet off the coast of Bougainville. Then they began darting from cloud to cloud, slipping ever closer to their target – thirty Japanese Zero fighters lined up wingtip to wingtip with ground crews moving amongst them.

So closely packed were the enemy planes that nearly all would be in range of the Marine fighters' machine guns. As the Corsairs swept down in formation, they came within 100 feet of the ground and 2,000

Missing Flier Wins Award For Heroism

For expert airmanship and aggressive fighting spirit throughout numerous combat missions in the South Pacific, First Lieutenant Robert L. Keister, U.S.M.C., has been awarded the Air Medal, his wife, Louise, 124 West Pueblo street, was informed last week.

Lieutenant Keister has been reported missing since November, 1943, after participating in a combat mission over Vella Lavella. He has been in the Marine Corps seven years and took part of his training here at the Marine Corps Air Station at Goleta. He is a Corsair fighter pilot and has been overseas since February, 1943.

According to the citation accompanying the medal, the lieutenant was credited with strafing a Jap airfield which "caused fires and explosions in a revetment area, destroying six and probably two other enemy fighter planes. Later, while taking part in a low-level raid, he directed his fire at hostile ground installations and succeeded in demolishing an anti-aircraft position."

The medal and citation were issued by Secretary of the Navy James Forrestal for the President.

Santa Barbara News Press, February 7, 1944

feet of their target. The men took the field completely by surprise and immediately opened fire. Lieutenant Keister ("Tailend Charlie" in the formation) was interviewed afterward and described his actions:

> "I opened fire on one side of the runway and just let the bullets eat their way right across the field into a group of six or eight, wavering my fire slightly by kicking my rudders. I officially demolished five."

When the men ceased firing, they were barely twenty feet off the ground. When they flew away from the field they could see smoke and flame from the Zeros for miles. It was estimated that an entire Japanese fighter squadron had been wiped out.

Mrs. Robert L. Keister receives the Air Medal and Citation awarded her husband, Lieutenant Keister, posthumously

By the time this account had been published in January 1944, Lieutenant Keister was listed as missing. The previous November 1, he had participated in a combat mission over Vella Lavella, part of the Solomon Islands, and had not returned to his base.

In June 1944 while still listed as missing, Lieutenant Keister's wife received the Air Medal and a citation on his behalf for his expert airmanship and aggressive fighting spirit. According to the citation, the lieutenant was credited with strafing a Japanese airfield causing fires and explosions in a revetment area and destroying at least six enemy planes. Later while he was part of a low-level raid, he directed his fire at enemy ground installations and succeeded in demolishing an anti-aircraft position.

The cause of his death has never been officially noted but his date of death is listed as November 2, 1944. Robert's name is listed on the Fort William McKinley Monument in Manila, the Philippines. Posthumously, he was also awarded the Purple Heart. A street at the Santa Barbara Airport was named in his honor.

Louise remained for a time in Santa Barbara. Apparently she never remarried and her death was noted in Orange County on December 27, 1988.

Santa Barbara News Press, March 15, 1944

LIEUTENANT FREDERICK PETER LOPEZ

Lt. Frederick P. Lopez

Frederick P. Lopez was known as Freddie. He was born in Carpinteria about 1922 to Jose and Candaleria Alvarado Lopez, the oldest of three boys. The family moved to Santa Barbara and eventually settled on Carpinteria Avenue. The boys were educated locally. Freddie graduated from Santa Barbara High School in 1940, and then completed one year of college. During his year in college, he enlisted as a private in the United States Army on Valentine's Day, 1941.

He attended the ordnance school at Aberdeen, Maryland, and then was sent to Fort Belvoir, Virginia, for officer training where he studied construction engineering. At age 19, he was commissioned a second lieutenant, the youngest officer at the time to graduate from the course.

In October 1944, Lieutenant Lopez was sent to Luxembourg with the 1258th Engineer Combat Battalion, a part of the Third Army. The battalion travelled through Germany and into Czechoslovakia and Austria. Most likely, the battalion's responsibility was to maintain and repair the airbases captured by Allied airborne forces.

By April 1945, World War II was nearing its end in Europe. The Allies had recently announced that future operations over Germany would focus on cleanup rather than strategic targets, effectively ending the air war. With the war so close to being over, the how and why of Lieutenant Lopez's death on April 26 in Germany are unknown. He was buried in the Lorraine American Cemetery in St. Avoid (Moselle), France. Lieutenant Lopez was awarded a Purple Heart and was honored by his brother Daniel on the National World War II Memorial Registry of Remembrances established in conjunction with the World War II Memorial in Washington DC.

Yearbook photograph of Frederick P. Lopez, a 1940 graduate of Santa Barbara High School

Besides his parents and brothers, Lieutenant Lopez was survived by his wife Consuelo (Connie) Torres and their daughter, Consuelo Linda. She was born August 1, 1944, in Santa Barbara just two months before Freddie left for Europe.

Youngest brother Daniel V. Lopez enlisted from Santa Barbara on April 19, 1945, as an Army private, soon after he had turned eighteen and six days before his brother was killed. Middle brother James Lopez enlisted in November 1942 at age seventeen. He joined the

Naval Reserve and trained to be a radio technician. He was on submarine duty in the Pacific when his older brother Freddie was killed.

A street at the Santa Barbara Airport bears Frederick Lopez's name, honoring his sacrifice during World War II. His family still lives in Santa Barbara and his grandson works for the City of Santa Barbara.

Capt. F. P. Lopez Killed in Action

Mrs. Frederick Peter Lopez of 328 Elizabeth St. has received word from the War Department that her husband was killed in action in Germany on April 26.

Capt. Lopez was a graduate of Santa Barbara High School in 1940 and attended Santa Barbara College for a year before enlisting in the Air Corps. He attended the ordnance school at Aberdeen, Md., after which he was sent to Fort Belvoir, Va., for officer training, where he studied construction engineering. He was the youngest officer ever to be graduated from this course.

Capt. Lopez went into Luxembourg in October, 1944, with the Third Army, and on through Germany into Czechoslovakia and Austria.

He is survived by a daughter, Linda, who is nine months old; his parents, Mr. and Mrs. Jose Lopez of 717 Carpinteria St., and two brothers, both of whom are in the service.

James Lopez, who belongs to the Naval Reserve, enlisted in November, 1942, at the age of 17, and is a CPO on submarine duty in the Pacific theater. He was a licensed amateur radio operator at 15, and had 14 months of training in radio and radar technique before going overseas.

Daniel Lopez is stationed at Camp Walters, Tex., having enlisted on April 19 of this year, just after his 18th birthday.

Santa Barbara News Press, May 10, 1945
(NOTE: Frederick Lopez achieved the rank of lieutenant, not captain)

LIEUTENANT DAVID CULVER LOVE

Lieutenant David C. Love

David was born May 19, 1922, to Harold and Mildred Culver Love. He was the oldest of three boys. He and his brothers attended local schools and graduated from Santa Barbara High School. In his senior year, David was class treasurer and a member of the ROTC. He graduated with the class of 1940, finishing his education in two years instead of three. At the outset, he did not want to go to college but wanted to work. He was hired as a mail carrier in Santa Barbara.

When he did decide to return to school, he entered a two-year forestry program at Mount Shasta in 1942. Upon completion, he took a job in San Bernardino County. He then went to work in the Angeles Forest.

He enlisted in the Army in 1943 as an aviation cadet and was initially trained at Santa Ana. Fellow high school friend Don Stillman said he was pleased to run into David at Santa Ana especially since David had a car. The two men would make frequent trips home to Santa Barbara to see their families and girlfriends. In December, David's engagement to his high school sweetheart Marilee Stevens was announced. The couple married the following February after David had completed gunnery school in Kingman, Arizona, and bombardier training in Deming, New Mexico.

Before he left for overseas duty, Lieutenant Love was stationed at Muroc Air Field. He was then sent to Wendling, England, and trained for combat missions over Germany. He was assigned to the 579th Bombardier Squadron of the 392nd Bomber Group. Before the war was over, the 392nd flew 285 missions with 4000 crewmembers and ground support from nearly 3000 personnel. About 21% of the group lost their lives.

One of the missions to suffer heavy losses took off on July 7, 1944, with forty-two aircraft. Flying in one of the planes headed for Bernberg Airfield in Germany was Second Lieutenant David Love. He was the bombardier on a B-24 Liberator aircraft nicknamed both the *Model T* and the *Bar-U* and piloted by Second Lieutenant William M. Milliken. Seven other crewmen were on board.

Apparently before reaching their target, the bomber group met heavy fighter opposition and flak. Before this day was over, the group would lose six aircraft and have five aircrews go missing. One of those planes shot down was carrying Lieutenant Love. There were no eyewitness accounts by returning crews on the loss of this aircraft and aircrew. A German report later reported the crash of this plane about 9:30 in the morning, and the finding of the dead crewmen two kilometers south of Egeln, near the city of Magdeburg, Germany.

LT. DAVID C. LOVE
Missing After Raid

There was one survivor of this ordeal, Co-Pilot Lieutenant Darnell who was blown out of the plane when it exploded while under enemy fighter attacks. His report indicated that most crewmembers were in their assigned positions when the plane suddenly blew up, and surmised all of them had been killed. He further related that the pilot and the radio operator were standing beside him and both were attempting to open the jammed bomb bay doors when the plane exploded sending him out of the forward section.

Originally the eight dead crewmembers were buried in the village cemetery at Egeln on July 9. They were later reburied at the National Cemetery in Ardennes. Second Lieutenant David C. Love has two grave markers, one in Ardennes, France, and a second one at the Neuville-En-Condroz Permanent Cemetery in Belgium. He was awarded the Purple Heart.

In 1948, the City of Santa Barbara named the streets of its airport after local aviators who died in World War II. David Love was honored with a street bearing his name.

Lt. David Love On Missing List

Lieutenant David C. Love of Goleta, son of Mrs. Mildred C Love and the late Harold G Love, has been missing since July 7 when he went out on a combat flight over Germany, it was reported Saturday by his mother.

The officer entered the Air Forces 17 months ago and was trained as a bombardier.

The lieutenant attended the local schools and took his preflight training at Santa Ana followed by gunnery school training at Kingman, Ariz. He completed bombardier training last February and following graduation from that training school married the former Marilee Stevens.

Before he left for overseas duty Lieutenant Love was stationed at Muroc Army Air Field and subsequently was sent across to an English base from which he flew out on bombing attacks in Axis occupied Europe and Germany.

**Santa Barbara News Press,
July 22, 1944**

Missing Officer Reported Killed

Lieutenant David C. Love, formerly reported missing in action, was killed on July 7, according to word received by his mother, Mrs. Mildred C. Love of Goleta, from the War department.

A bombardier, Lieutenant Love was killed over Germany. He attended local schools, and prior to enlisting was employed by the U.S. Forest service. He entered the Army in February, 1943, and graduated from the Deming Air Field, N. Mex., the following year.

In addition to his mother, he is survived by his widow, Marilee, of Ontario, and two brothers, George, also in the service, and Dick, who is awaiting call in the Army Air Forces.

**Santa Barbara News Press,
October 31, 1944**

LIEUTENANT ANDREW RANSALIER MACFARLAND

Andrew R. MacFarland, known as Andy, was the only child of Ransalier and Ruth MacFarland, though he did have half siblings from his parents' previous marriages. Andy was born in Santa Barbara on March 23, 1922. He attended local schools and graduated from Santa Barbara High School in 1940. While in high school, Andy was a member of the Aviation Club and ROTC. He enrolled in Santa Barbara State College and took classes in physics. He was also interested in mechanical engineering and hoped to attend Cal Tech after he was discharged from the military.

Lt. Andrew R. MacFarland

While attending college, Andy met Barbara Chapman. They fell in love and married January 11, 1944, in the Old Mission, Santa Barbara where Barbara had been baptized twenty-two years earlier.

Andy had joined the Air Corps June 6, 1942, and had reported to duty the following March. According to Barbara, he joined the Air Corps because "he wanted to learn to fly, become a pilot, and do his part in helping his country win the war." He was first stationed in Santa Ana, and after the initial drills and testing, he was selected for pilot training. He trained in Ontario, then in Merced, and finally at Muroc Air Force Base (now Edwards Air Force Base). Flying the B-24 Liberator aircraft, he completed his training in Douglas, Arizona (now a general aviation airport), where he earned his pilot's wings and achieved the rank of second lieutenant.

Lt. and Mrs. Andrew MacFarland on their wedding day, January 11, 1944

The service sent him first to India, then to China. He became a member of the 373rd Bomber Squadron and flew as co-pilot to Second Lieutenant John A. Bigelow. Their squadron was assigned to the 308th Bomb Group of the Fourteenth Air Force, whose responsibilities were varied. The planes and their crew made many trips over The Hump to India to obtain gasoline, oil, bombs, spare parts, and other items needed to prepare for and then to sustain its combat operations. The 308th Group supported Chinese ground forces. It attacked airfields, coal yards, docks, oil refineries, and fuel dumps in French Indochina. It mined rivers and ports and attacked Japanese shipping in the East China Sea, Formosa Strait, South China Sea, and the Gulf of Tonkin.

When he was not flying, Andy enjoyed hiking the hillsides near his base. Sometimes he hiked with a Chinese pilot friend, other times with fellow crewmembers. He would often send tiny photos of his jaunts home to Barbara.

Santa Barbara's Fallen Aviators of World War II

On Andy's last mission September 28, 1944, he was the co-pilot of a B-24 that began experiencing engine trouble shortly after take-off. The crew had to turn back to Luliang Base but the plane crashed before reaching it. Four of the crew survived but the other six did not.

Barbara was pregnant with their son when she received a telegram notifying her of Andy's death. The notification was followed by a visit from two officers who came to her home. The bodies of all the crewmembers were recovered and a simple service was conducted by a Protestant chaplain for these fallen heroes. Andy's body was finally returned to Santa Barbara in late 1948 or early 1949 and buried in the family plot in the Santa Barbara Cemetery.

After his death, Second Lieutenant MacFarland was awarded a Purple Heart and the Asiatic-Pacific Theater Service Campaign Ribbon with one Bronze Star for the China Campaign.

He also received the Air Medal along with this citation:

Santa Barbara News Press,
October 29, 1944

> *"For meritorious achievement in aerial flight as pilot. They participated in more than eighty hours of combat flight from bases in China and India in heavy bombardment type aircraft from 20 July to 27 September 1944. Although fire from enemy ground guns and hostile aircraft was encountered on many flights, they carried out their missions with cool determination and are credited with having inflicted heavy losses of material and personnel on the enemy. They carried out attacks against communications centers, troop concentrations, ocean vessels, warehouses and supply dumps throughout the vast expanses of China, Indo-China, Burma and Thailand. Many missions were flown through adverse weather and over mountains and poorly charted areas. The courage and determination that these officers demonstrated in combat reflect great credit upon themselves and upon the Army Air Force."*

Young Andrew Bruce was born four months later. Barbara sensed her husband would have been a wonderful father to their son had he lived. She watched how Andy had treated his young nephew with such care and attention as he did his family and hers. She remembers her lieutenant as a caring and loving man who was well liked by his peers. "My parents liked him too."

Barbara later married Ray Andrew Wessinger and they had a son, Ray Alan, who was born in December 1951 in Pasadena. Barbara and her husband eventually made their home in Hawaii where he died in 1996. Their son passed away in 2008. Barbara still lives in Hawaii and her son, Andrew Bruce, resides in Ohio.

Andrew MacFarland is remembered for his service on the World War II Memorial at Santa Barbara High School. A street at the Santa Barbara Airport is named in his honor.

STAFF SERGEANT ROBERT K. MARXMILLER

Robert and his twin brother, William David, were born to Chester and Irma Mae Smithley Marxmiller on May 1, 1922, in San Francisco. They were Chester and Irma's only children.

Robert K. Marxmiller in his high school graduation photograph, 1942

The Marxmiller family moved to Santa Barbara where the boys attended Santa Barbara High School. While in high school Robert, known as Bob, was active in a Hi-Y Club and joined ROTC attaining the rank of first lieutenant. Bob graduated with the Class of 1942. He had a job in the circulation department of the local newspaper while enrolled at Santa Barbara State College. Prior to his enlistment, Bob worked for Southern California Edison.

Bob enlisted in the Army Air Corps on May 12, 1942, and the following October started training at Kelly Field in San Antonio. He saw training service at Lowry Field in Denver where he graduated from the Armament Department, then attended gunnery school in Laredo, Texas, where he earned his gunner's wings. His last assignment before going overseas was in Alamogordo, New Mexico, in early 1944. Alamogordo Army Air Field served as the training base for over twenty different groups, primarily training in B-17s, B-24s, and B-29s. Usually these groups trained at the airfield for about six months, preparing for combat in the Pacific or European Theaters.

Sergeant Marxmiller was sent to Lavenham Airbase in Suffolk County, England, as a member of the 839th Bomber Squadron attached to the 487th Bomber Group. The 487th had been assigned to Lavenham since September 22, 1943, and would remain there until November 7, 1945. A total of 185 missions were flown by crews of the 487th using both B-24 and B-17 aircraft. Over the twenty-five month period, more than twenty-two aircraft would be destroyed and eighteen damaged. The 487th began combat in May 1944, bombing airfields in France in preparation for the invasion of Normandy; then they assaulted coastal defenses, road junctions, bridges, and locomotives during the invasion.

The *Box Car* crew, with Sergeant Marxmiller front row, last person on right

Floyd Schwab was the pilot for his eight-member crew assigned to a B-24 Liberator dubbed *Box Car*. On June 7, 1944, *Box Car* took off from Lavenham on its first mission with seven of the eight crew members on board. The target was the Montjean Bridge held by the enemy near the airfield at Angers, France.

The ball turret gunner on board was Staff Sergeant Marxmiller, probably the smallest member of the crew. This gunner had to sit in a tiny space with his back and head against the rear wall of the turret and his legs held in mid-air by two footrests on the front wall. This position allowed his eyes to be roughly level with a pair of machine guns which extended through the entire turret located on either side of the gunner. Because the space was so small, the triggers were pulled by a cable attached to the guns and a handle near the front of the turret.

On the return flight to England just before eight in the evening, *Box Car* was hit by enemy fire near Rennes, France, sending the plane into a steep dive. Within a minute of being struck, the plane exploded, the wings tore away, and the fuselage broke apart. Three men were still in the nose of the plane and Staff Sergeant Marxmiller in the ball turret when the plane caught fire. Three others, including the pilot, were able to bail out before it exploded and were captured on the ground. The pilot and the tail gunner were taken to a prison hospital in Rennes and treated for second and third degree burns. The waist gunner was captured and later released. It was the only aircraft of the 487th to be lost that day.

Robert Marxmiller, B-24 Gunner, Is Missing in Action

Staff Sergeant Robert Marxmiller, 22-year-old son of Mr. and Mrs. C. G. Marxmiller, 10 Mission Park drive, has been missing in action over France since June 7, according to a War department dispatch just received by his parents.

Marxmiller was first gunner aboard a B-24, and went into training in 1942. Last March he flew home from a New Mexico camp to spend 24 hours of a 48-hour leave before going to England.

The young gunner was a News-Press circulation department employe and a student at Santa Barbara State college before entering the service.

Santa Barbara News Press, June 27, 1944

Staff Sergeant Robert K. Marxmiller was buried in the Brittany American Cemetery in St. James, France. He was awarded the Air Medal and a Purple Heart posthumously for his service. In 1948, a street at the Santa Barbara Airport was named for Robert Marxmiller.

The Marxmiller family suffered two more tragedies after Bob's death. Irma Marxmiller passed away in Santa Barbara in 1948. Six years later on May 4, Bob's twin brother William, the Santa Barbara Fire District Warden, was in his fire truck responding to a fire near Refugio when he suffered fatal injuries in a vehicle collision. Chester Marxmiller relocated to San Diego and died there in 1967.

Sgt. Marxmiller is buried in Brittany American Cemetery, St. James, France

LIEUTENANT (J.G.) EARL ALDER MCALLISTER

Earl Alder McAllister was born May 6, 1922, in Provo, Utah, to John Wells and Mary Myrl McAllister. He was the middle of five children. His father had trained as an opera singer in Chicago so music was a rich part of the McAllister home. John supported his family by working with bands in the Midwest before becoming a music teacher for Brigham Young University in Provo.

Lt. (j.g.) Earl McAllister

The family moved west in 1928 when John was offered a teaching position at a high school in Santa Maria. Two years later he became the band leader for Santa Barbara High School and the family moved into town. They lived in five different homes in the twelve years they remained in Santa Barbara until they returned to Utah. All but the youngest two McAllister children graduated from Santa Barbara High School. While attending Santa Barbara High, Earl played the trombone and, as a senior, was the drum major for the school's marching band. He also began to date his classmate Margaret (Peggy) Hamilton whom he later married.

Earl was the first of his brothers to join the service; he chose the Naval Air Corps so he could learn to fly. Training first took him to San Francisco and then back east to Pensacola, Florida.

As part of Fighting Squadron 82, Lieutenant McAllister was assigned to the USS *Bennington,* a 27,000 ton aircraft carrier built in a New York shipyard and launched in February 1944. Training for the squadron on its new aircraft carrier took place in Atlantic City, then Oceana, Virginia, and finally on a shakedown cruise to Trinidad, British West Indies.

On New Year's Day 1945, the ship headed for Japan through the Panama Canal. Most of January was spent in the Hawaiian Islands where the squadron engaged in training exercises before becoming part of Admiral Marc Mitscher's famed Task Force 58. The Task Force consisted of the commander's flagship USS *Lexington*, five other aircraft carriers including the USS *Enterprise*, six light aircraft carriers, and a host of supporting ships. The role of the Task Force was to seek out and destroy the Japanese fleet and naval air forces. In 1945, it supported the amphibious landings at Iwo Jima and Okinawa, fought off Japanese kamikaze air attacks, and struck airfields and strategic targets in Formosa and Japan.

Silver Star

The first strike by the Task Force was against Tokyo, then in rapid succession, Chichi Jima, Iwo Jima, and Tokyo again. The enemy was hit at Kure, Kyushu, and Shikoku; Okinawa was invaded with support from Squadron 82 which inflicted many deadly strikes including the sinking of the *Yamato*, the largest Japanese warship.

Flying the Hellcat Fighter, Lieutenant McAllister participated in twelve raids including those over Tokyo and Iwo Jima. On March 19, 1945, his plane was hit by enemy fire during a strafing attack on Kochi Air Field on the island of Shikoku. His airplane was torn apart during a high speed dive towards the airfield before it crashed into the sea. Lieutenant McAllister was declared Missing in Action. The family was notified by letter that the airman was missing.

Lieutenant McAllister's family later learned that a Japanese fisherman had found Earl's body floating in the sea. Apparently Earl had managed to escape the plane before it crashed. After the war, a Japanese farmer came forward to let authorities know that he had buried the body of an American in his field.

The body was retrieved, identified as that of Lieutenant Earl McAllister, and reburied in Honolulu. A second letter was sent to Earl's parents asking if they wanted the body to remain in Hawaii or sent home. They asked that it be sent home, and their son was buried in the McAllister family plot in Manti, Utah.

About a month before Earl was shot down, Peggy had given birth to their daughter, Linda. Sadly, he never saw his daughter before he died. Peggy married again in November 1946. She and Lawrence Cortez had several children. Earl's daughter, Linda, took her stepfather's last name until she married in 1970.

Lieutenant McAllister was awarded the Silver Star Medal accompanied by the following citation:

> *"For conspicuous gallantry and intrepidity as pilot of a Fighter Plane attached to the U.S.S. BENNINGTON in action against enemy Japanese forces in the Kure Harbor area on March 19, 1945. Participating in a seven-plane fighter sweep over enemy airfields, Lieutenant, Junior Grade, McAllister boldly fought his plane through terrific hostile antiaircraft fire to launch a vigorous strafing and rocket-projectile strike against an enemy carrier and, plunging to the attack with determined aggressiveness, contributed materially to the infliction of severe damage on the vital Japanese ship. By his brilliant airmanship and great personal valor in the face of grave peril, Lieutenant, Junior Grade, McAllister upheld the highest traditions of the United States Naval Service."*
>
> *For the President,*
>
> *James Forrestal*
> *Secretary of the Navy*

Santa Barbara News Press, April 12, 1945

LIEUTENANT FRED CHADWICK MCCLOSKEY

Fred Chadwick McCloskey was known as Chad. He was born on May 26, 1922, and was the older of two sons born to Fred and Dorothy Tinker McCloskey. His family farmed. His grandfather Tinker had come from Michigan and operated a wheat farm on Hollister Avenue in Goleta. According to a boyhood friend of Chad's, it was here that the aviator and his brother grew up.

Chad attended Santa Barbara High School where he was a member of the same ROTC company as Andrew MacFarland, another honored aviator. Chad graduated in June 1940. While in high school he met and courted Peggy Lou Welsh. He enlisted in the Army Air Corps as a cadet on March 18, 1943, and was sent initially to Santa Ana. On October 23, he and Peggy were married in the little chapel on the air base in Merced where he was training as a P-38 fighter pilot.

Lt. Fred C. McCloskey

He earned his wings and was commissioned a second lieutenant. In early 1944, Chad completed flight training in advanced single engine aircraft at an Army Air Force pilot school in Arizona.

He was sent to Italy where he was promoted to first lieutenant. There, he was attached to the 27th Fighter Squadron of the 13th Air Force and was appointed an assistant flight leader. The 27th was the top-scoring unit of the 1st Fighter Group in World War II with eighty-three of its pilots credited with over 176 victories.

Lt. Fred C. McCloskey on the wing of his aircraft

While on leave in early 1945, Chad visited Rome where he purchased rosaries for his wife and her grandmother and had them blessed by Pope Pius XII.

Upon his return to active duty, he was killed in combat over Italy on January 16, 1945, just a week after his promotion and appointment. In a letter he had written to his wife before his death, he told her he had already completed seventeen missions. In recognition of Lieutenant McCloskey's courage and leadership, his fellow fliers had christened him "Fearless Freddie." His body was returned to the States after the war and buried in Goleta Cemetery.

Santa Barbara's Fallen Aviators of World War II

Lieutenant McCloskey was awarded the Air Medal and Bronze Oak Leaf Cluster posthumously for meritorious achievement in aerial flight. His widow received his medals and a letter from Major General William Shedd of the Ninth Service Command which read in part:

> *"It has been a source of inspiration to me to learn of your husband's exceptionally meritorious achievements in action against the enemy which have merited these awards. His courage, determination, and devotion to duty must be a source of comfort and pride to you at this time."*

Chad McCloskey is remembered for his service to his country on the World War II Memorial at Santa Barbara High School. A street at the Santa Barbara Airport is named in his honor. In April 1946 Chad's widow, Peggy, married William C. Buckley.

Goleta Cemetery, Goleta, California

Santa Barbara News Press,
February 2, 1945

Sergeant Nicholas John Mesa

Sgt. Nicholas Mesa

Nicholas (Nick) Mesa was born May 7, 1921, under the name of Nicholas John Franco. However, he was raised by Frank Mesa (whose name Nick assumed) and Esperanza Garcia.

Nick enlisted in the US Army Air Force out of Hawaii on October 14, 1938. He married Ilone Slebiss, a local Santa Barbara woman. Their son, John Anthony, was born in Santa Barbara on June 13, 1942.

Nick was a sergeant and an aerial photographer in the 11th Air Force. He was assigned to the 21st Squadron of the 28th Bomber Group. The 11th was headquartered in Alaska and provided air defense for the territory. It also engaged in combat operations primarily in the Aleutian Islands and the northern Pacific after the bombing of Dutch Harbor in the eastern Aleutian Islands by the Japanese.

Primarily an air war, the Aleutian Campaign was the only World War II operation fought on North American soil and, because of the remoteness of the islands and the difficulties of the weather and terrain, it took nearly a year for the large U.S. force to eject the enemy and reoccupy the islands. During that time, the 11th Air Force flew 297 missions and dropped 3,662 tons of bombs.

Attu Island became the base for the 28th Bomber Group and over 1,500 sorties were flown against the Kuriles before the end of the war, including the Japanese base of Paramushiru at the southern tip of the Kamchatka Peninsula. Paramushiru was the target on August 11, 1943, when Nick and his crew mates took off in their B-24 from Attu. The pilot was Captain Harrell Ringo Hoffman. On board were nine other crew members including Sergeant Mesa, the photographer.

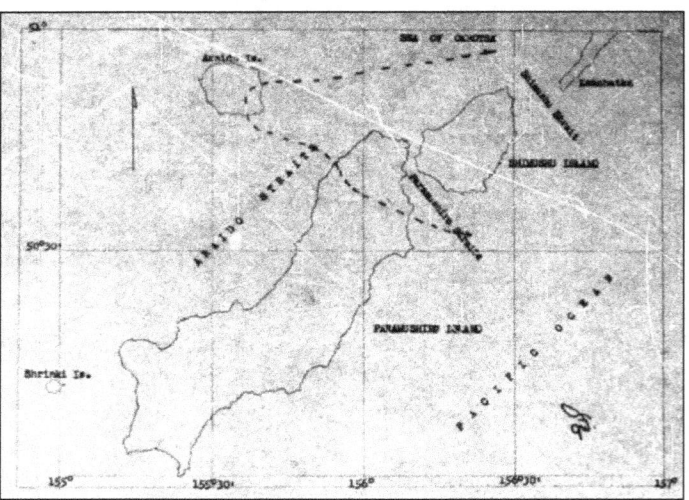

The operational area within which Sgt. Mesa was flying at the time of his death

The plane reached 12,000 feet over the Paramushiru Strait and the Kurile Islands when suddenly two enemy aircraft closed in on the B-24. The crew attempted outside contact with radioman Staff Sergeant Andrew F. Krempuach who saw the plane crash. At the outset, the crew was listed as Missing in Action. Later it was determined that no one survived, though the final determination was not made until January 1946.

Santa Barbara's Fallen Aviators of World War II

For the remainder of the war, the 11th Air Force flew bombing and reconnaissance missions from Attu and Shemya Islands against Japanese military installations in the northern Kurile Islands. American planners had briefly contemplated an invasion of northern Japan from the Aleutians during the fall of 1943, but rejected the idea as too risky and impractical.

Nick J. Mesa was memorialized at the National Memorial Cemetery of the Pacific, Honolulu, Hawaii, and posthumously awarded the Air Medal and Purple Heart. In 1946, a stone was placed in the Riverside National Cemetery in memory of Nick. Later his son had a stone erected to honor his father in Arlington National Cemetery. In 2004, when the World War II Memorial was dedicated in Washington DC, Nick's son, John, again honored the father he never knew by listing him on the National World War II Memorial Registry of Remembrances.

Sgt. Nicholas J. Mesa

Airman Missing Following Raid

News of the first Santa Barbara casualty in the Paramushiro battle area was revealed Wednesday with the arrival of a telegram from Washington, D.C., which announced that Sergeant

SERGEANT MESA
Missing in Action

Nick J. Mesa is missing in that theater of operations against the Japanese homeland.

The flier, an aerial photographer, is the husband of Mrs. Ilona Mesa, 217 South Milpas street. The telegram reported he had been unaccounted for since August 11.

According to a letter received from Corporal F. Patterson, buddy-in-arms of Mesa, the sergeant went out with a flight from an Alaskan base. His plane did not return. This letter arrived before the official message came from the adjutant general in Washington.

Sergeant Mesa has been in the Army Air forces since before Pearl Harbor. Only recently friends in Santa Barbara had received mail from him in which he mentioned that he expected to be home shortly on a furlough.

Awaiting him at home besides his wife is a 14-months-old son, John Anthony, whom the flying photographer had never seen. The flier is the adopted son of Mrs. Esperanto Garcia of 40 East Valley road.

Santa Barbara New Press,
August 23, 1945

STAFF SERGEANT JOHN EMIL MILLER

John was born in Santa Barbara on June 14, 1923, the fourth of eight children born to Benjamin and Marguerite Cone Miller. His father was a farmer who grew fruit in Carpinteria. He also did road work as a laborer. John's parents divorced and his mother went to live in the San Diego area. John stayed with his dad.

John did not finish high school. Instead he quit after his junior year and began working on a local ranch before enlisting in the Army Air Corps on October 6, 1942. He trained as a waist gunner on B-17s and earned his staff sergeant's stripes. He was assigned to the Eighth Air Force stationed in England as part of the 305th Bomber Group.

Sgt. John E. Miller

The primary duty of a waist gunner was to look for and defend against enemy fighters. When the waist gunner had an enemy plane in sight, he had to make sure that he was looking through his machine gun sight at exactly the proper angle or his aim would be off. The waist gunner also had the responsibility to call out fighter positions so that the other gunners knew where to expect the next attack and the navigator could log the number of enemy aircraft involved in the attack. If an enemy aircraft were hit, the waist gunner would also call this out for the navigator to log. He also reported damage done to his plane and would assist the flight engineer in making repairs to the aircraft while in flight. It did not take the Germans long to figure out that the best way to attack a B-17 was from dead ahead, thus avoiding attack from the gunners.

A crew photograph of *Sizzle*, a B-17, to which Sgt. Miller was assigned on the day of his death

When the 305th Bomber Group first came to England, its targets were initially harbors, docks, and shipyards in France, Germany, and the Low Countries. By the latter part of 1943, the 305th began deeper penetration into enemy territory to strike heavy industry. On October 14, 1943, the 1st and 3rd Bombardment Divisions of the 305th left Chelveston, England, for a second attack on the German ball-bearing plants at Schweinfurt, Germany. Almost 230 heavy bombers attacked the city and its ball-bearing plants. The attacks were successful enough that the Germans were forced to reorganize their bearing industry. However, using a great number of fighter planes, the Germans also put up a fierce fight and shot down sixty U.S. aircraft, including the one carrying Sergeant Miller.

Santa Barbara's Fallen Aviators of World War II

Second Lieutenant Douglas L. Murdock was the pilot in command of the B-17, nicknamed *Sizzle*, with a crew of ten. Sergeant Miller was the bombardier on this mission. As a result of these heavy losses, daylight bombing against strategic targets deep into Germany was discontinued briefly.

John's father was notified that his son had gone missing. Later, Sergeant Miller was awarded the Air Medal for his actions during the war. John was interred at the Santa Barbara Cemetery on April 29, 1950. John Miller's service is honored on the Carpinteria High School World War II Memorial.

Ironically, John's good friend Bernard Snow, who enlisted with John on the same day in the Army Air Corps back in 1942 and later hooked up with him in England, was also reported as missing in this pulverizing raid. He survived and was taken prisoner by the Germans. In June 1945, he was liberated and returned to Carpinteria to live.

Staff Sergeants John E. Miller and Bernard E. Snow. *Santa Barbara News Press,* October 28, 1943

Santa Barbara Cemetery, Santa Barbara, California

Lieutenant William Lynn Moffett

William (Bill) was the middle of nine children born to Leander and Rose Gomm Moffett. His oldest sister, Rose, was born in Wyoming before the family moved to Cassia County, Idaho, and then Cambridge, Idaho, where William was born in 1920, and his father was a farmer.

Lt. William L. Moffett, in 1942

Bill's niece, Sherrie Gardner, remembers her uncle as, " ... a favorite in our family. One of nine children with our mother being the oldest, he was so fun loving and we heard many stories of what a great guy he was."

Bill enlisted in the Army Air Corps out of Salt Lake City as a cadet on September 27, 1941. He had completed two years of college at the University of Wyoming at the time of his enlistment. He and his brother Leonard had spent two previous years in Santa Barbara and Bill had planned to transfer to Santa Barbara State College before he enlisted. He trained in California and graduated in August 1942 from the Victorville Bomber School, second in his class. From there, he and his crew were sent to Miami, Florida, and then on to Africa.

He rose to the rank of lieutenant and saw action as a bombardier on the B-24 at Tobruk, Tripoli, Bizerte, Tunis, and Pantelleria. During World War II, more than 45,000 bombardiers were trained and entrusted with one of the nation's most closely kept secrets, the Norden bombsight. The Pilot Training Manual described the duties of the bombardier stating that,

> "When the bombardier takes over the airplane for the run on the target, he is in absolute command. He will tell you what he wants done, and until he tells you 'Bombs Away', his word is law."

Bill was killed June 13, 1943, following a military mission over Sicily. Lieutenant Moffett was a veteran of more than 200 flying hours. He was one of several dozen flyers who had graced the cover of the July 26, 1943, issue of *Life* magazine.

According to his best friend and flying buddy Lieutenant Dave Gandin of Los Angeles (who was also featured on the magazine cover), William's last words were the same as he said before each raid: *"Come on, Dave, let's go out and fight the war."*

The cover of *Life* magazine, July 26, 1943, showcased 8th Air Force Bombers, including Lt. William Moffett

After Bill's death, Dave wrote the following to the family:

> *"I knew Bill as my finest friend. We had roomed, tented, and roughed it on the desert together. Together we had fought the same war in the same airplane for the same purpose – it's strange without him right now. With all my heart I go and fight for Bill each day…"*

Santa Barbara's Fallen Aviators of World War II

Lieutenant Gandin also gave the details of Bill's death. Bill was the squadron bombardier who was flying in the lead plane of another crew. Dave's crew was leading the next element. Bill's crew made a run on the target, destroying hangars and dispersing aircraft. On the way home Bill's B-24 Liberator plane suddenly plunged into the Mediterranean Sea. Apparently it had been damaged while strafing its targets. No one survived the crash and no bodies were recovered. Bill's name is listed on the North African Memorial outside of Tunis, Tunisia.

Squadron Bombardier Lt. William L. Moffett, pictured above, center

Lieutenant Moffett was honored at ceremonies conducted at Ontario Army Air Field. The commanding officer presented his parents with the Distinguished Flying Cross, Air Medal, Purple Heart, and two Oak Leaf clusters. The Distinguished Flying Cross came with a notation stating that the flier was honored for participation in aerial flights on combat missions in the Middle East:

> *"As Squadron-Bombardier Lieutenant Moffett often demonstrated unusual skill and initiative in leading entire formations of bombers on many of the most successful attacks yet on enemy objectives."*

In 1948 when the City of Santa Barbara named the streets of its airport for local aviators who lost their lives during World War II, William Moffett was honored with a street bearing his name. Although Bill Moffett's time in Santa Barbara was brief, he truly became one of the hometown heroes of the Great World War.

His best friend, Dave Gandin, became an Air Force captain. During the Korean War, he was a crew member of a B-29A Superfortress Bomber slated for a combat mission when it crashed into the sea upon take-off. No one survived.

***Santa Barbara News Press*, August 2, 1943**

ENSIGN ARTHUR PAUL MOLLENHAUER

Arthur (Art) Paul Mollenhauer was the second of four sons born to Paul and Augusta Kuglitsch Mollenhauer on August 7, 1924, in Cook County, Illinois. His older brother, Paul, Jr., and younger brother, Robert (Bob), were also born in Cook County. The family moved to California before the birth of Clarence on September 24, 1928.

To support his large family, Paul operated a barbershop in Santa Barbara. The family moved away for a time, living in Oakland and later in Hayward. Then in September 1937, Paul and Augusta were granted a divorce in Reno. Augusta moved to San Francisco where she worked as a waitress. Paul moved back to Santa Barbara where Art graduated from Santa Barbara High School in 1941, despite the fact he left school six months before the term was over and enlisted in the Naval Reserves in January 1942. While attending high school, Art was a second lieutenant in the ROTC.

Ensign Arthur Mollenhauer

After completing boot camp in San Diego, Art was sent to Navy Pier in Chicago for a year where he earned an aviation machinist's mate second class rating. He was then transferred to the aviation branch of the Navy in January 1943 to learn to fly. He received his primary flight training at the Naval Air Station at Pasco, Washington. He was transferred to Corpus Christi, Texas, for advanced flight training and received his Navy "wings" and a commission as an ensign in the Naval Reserve.

Navy Cross Ensign Mollenhauer went on to Florida where he married Eleanor Weidner in 1943, then transferred to San Diego to await his orders. Eleanor returned to Santa Barbara and worked as a secretary for a van and storage company. In October of 1944 Eleanor and her father-in-law received word that Art had become the Navy's newest ace pilot – Santa Barbara's first ever. He was flying an F6F Hellcat based on the carrier USS *Intrepid* when he shot down five Japanese planes over Formosa (now Taiwan) on October 12, 1944. Ironically, it was the first time Ensign Mollenhauer had ever seen an enemy plane in the air, and he bagged five!

The F6F Hellcat plane was first introduced into the war in mid-1943. Twelve thousand five hundred planes were produced carrying six 50-caliber machine guns each. They could travel at speeds up to 376 mph. When camouflaged and viewed from above, the plane was to resemble the color of the sea; viewed from below, it resembled the color of the sky. The planes were built specifically to counter the Japanese Zeros and the Hellcat was nicknamed the "ace maker" (and so it was). The kill ratio was 11:1!

The F6F Hellcat, the type of aircraft flown by Lt. Art Mollenhauer

After Ensign Mollenhauer's heroic efforts, he was interviewed by Philip S. Meisler, war correspondent for the *Baltimore Sun*. Meisler wrote the following:

> "The 21 year old pilot from Santa Barbara, Calif. saw his first enemy plane in the air when he was cutting in over the Formosa coast. He shot it down. He saw his second enemy plane 10 seconds later and shot that one down too. From then on it was just a case of seeing his third, fourth, and fifth Japanese planes and knocking them out of the plane-filled sky. 'They just kept flying in front of me and I just kept my finger on the gun button,' Mollenhauer told me in the ready room after the battle."

A few days later, Moe (as he was familiarly known) came in for a night landing on the *Intrepid*. He had just made the deck when another plane also came in and its wing scraped his cockpit, smashing the windshield and knocking Moe out. He took four stitches in the head then announced he was ready to do battle again. This time it was a strike against the Philippine province of Leyte in support of ground operations.

Perhaps this was his last mission as, seventeen days later, Ensign Arthur P. Mollenhauer was reported missing over the Pacific. His young wife was the one to receive the news. He was awarded a Purple Heart, the Air Medal, and the Navy Cross Medal, the highest medal awarded by the US Department of the Navy and the second highest award for valor.

The latter was awarded by the President of the United States with this citation:

> "For extraordinary heroism in operations against the enemy while serving as Pilot of a carrier-based Navy Fighter Plane in Fighting Squadron Eighteen (VF-18), attached to the U.S.S. INTREPID (CV-11), during a raid by carrier-based planes on northern Formosa on 12 October 1944. Ensign Mollenhauer flew his fighter-bomber through intensive anti-aircraft fire to carry out an effective bombing attack on a large and important enemy aircraft hangar. During this attack, he boldly engaged a superior force of Japanese airplanes and, despite the great odds against him, shot down five enemy craft. He not only contributed to the complete rout of the enemy formation, but, in two instances, saved the lives of his teammates. Ensign Mollenhauer's outstanding courage, daring airmanship and devotion to duty were in keeping with the highest traditions of the United States Naval Service. He gallantly gave his life for his country."

Santa Barbara News Press, Feb. 25, 1945

Art Mollenhauer was truly a hero; he was remembered on the monument at Fort William McKinley in Manila, the Philippines. In 1948 the Santa Barbara City Council named the streets of the airport for local aviators who lost their lives during World War II. Arthur Mollenhauer was honored with a street bearing his name. Paul Mollenhauer was proud of his son's achievements, and his barbershop on Hollister (now State Street) was filled with mementoes of Art's achievements.

AVIATION CADET FELIX LEE MOON, JR.

Felix Jr. was called June (short for Junior) by his parents and family. He was born April 5, 1928, in Oklahoma City to Felix Lee and Marjorie Hansen Moon. His younger sister, Noreen, was also born in Oklahoma City.

Cadet Felix Lee Moon, Jr.

The family moved to California and Felix graduated from Carpinteria High School in 1946. He was too young to have served in the Second World War, but as soon as he was eighteen he enlisted in the service, much to the dismay of his mother. He chose the Army Air Corps and served two years stateside and a year in Alaska before his discharge.

He really wanted to be a pilot so he reentered the service in the newly created United States Air Force to learn how to fly. The stipulation to earn his wings was he had to have either two years of college or pass an entrance exam. Since he only had a high school diploma, he took the exam and passed it. He was then accepted as a cadet.

Felix reported to Perrin Air Force Base in Denton, Texas, in October 1949 as a member of Class 50-F. Near the end of his training, Felix and his instructor were killed near Colbert, Oklahoma, when the engine failed in their T-6 training aircraft. Felix was in the pilot seat. Unfortunately, the plane had reached an altitude of less than 500 feet so parachuting was not an option. The plane landed in a grove of trees and neither man survived the crash.

Reports of Felix's death on March 8, 1950, listed him as a resident of Idaho when he died. According to Noreen, the Moon family did not actually live there; they were merely in Idaho (near Jerome) to help a family member work his farm. They were returning to California and their home in Carpinteria when they received word of Felix's death.

Felix's training was in preparation for the forthcoming Korean conflict. At the time of his death, he was four weeks shy of his twenty-second birthday and not married. He was buried in the Carpinteria Cemetery where his parents were later laid to rest. His

The T-6 Trainer, the type of aircraft flown by Cadet Felix Moon when he was killed

body had been brought from Texas accompanied by a military guard; his headstone was furnished by the Air Force.

Noreen loved her big brother who was a kind and caring person. She described him as very bright and a high achiever. Interestingly, Noreen also acquired her pilot's license at the tender age of seventeen. Noreen's husband is a World War II and Korean War veteran, and they have a grandson now in the U.S. Army serving in the Iraq/Afghanistan conflicts.

Cadet Felix L. Moon, Jr., in flight gear

Carpinteria Cemetery, Carpinteria, California

LIEUTENANT ROBERT WILLIAM NEWMAN

Robert W. Newman was known as Bob. He was the "big brother" to his three sisters, Betty, Marian, and Virginia. Bob was born January 23, 1917, in Santa Barbara to Rolla (Raul) and Frances Gill Newman. In 1920, the Newmans owned a home on Hollister Avenue, and Raul was a nurse for a private family. After the youngest two girls were born, the family lived on West Mission Street where they owned a home.

Lt. Robert W. Newman

The Newman children attended Santa Barbara schools. Bob graduated from Santa Barbara High School in 1935. While a student, he played football and tennis. Bob spent one year in college before attending the Admiral Farragut Academy in New Jersey. The academy was founded in 1933 as a college preparatory school and military academy; later the school expanded its program to a campus in St. Petersburg, Florida, before shuttering the New Jersey campus in 1994. Two of the twelve men who have walked on the moon graduated from the New Jersey campus of the Admiral Farragut Academy.

According to Virginia, Bob wanted to enter the Naval Academy, but because he was too old, he instead returned to California to attend a flight training school in San Luis Obispo. He enrolled with his best friend, Gil Macy. They both graduated and then Bob went on to Texas A&M.

Upon graduation from college, he enlisted in the Army Air Corps in July 1940, and was sent to Clark Air Field in the Philippines in 1941. He was assigned to the 3rd Pursuit Squadron of the 24th Pursuit Group as a second lieutenant pilot flying the P-35A. The P-35 had the distinction of being the first "modern" American all-metal fighter plane with a single seat, an enclosed cockpit, and retractable landing gear. It was designed by the Seversky Company, founded by Alexander De Seversky, a Russian émigré who defected to the United States in 1918 after a career as a fighter pilot.

The P-35A aircraft, similar to the one flown by Lt. Robert Newman

Despite its early promise, the plane soon became outdated. It lacked sufficient armament protection, did not have a self-sealing fuel tank, and its lateral stability was mediocre, making some maneuvers dangerous. As a matter of fact, Lieutenant Newman had a non-combat mishap in July 1941 when he landed his plane, hit a sand pile, and plopped his plane in a hole. Damage was limited to the right landing gear, the right wing and flap, and the propeller. Bob was not injured.

The P-35A had a short combat career as it was easily overtaken by more capable enemy aircraft. After Pearl Harbor was bombed, the Japanese targeted the Philippines and swept

The Bataan Death March

many Allied aircraft from the skies overhead. By December 12, 1941, only eight P-35As were still in flying condition, and they were soon re-designated as RP-35As, meaning they were unfit for combat.

By effectively neutralizing US air and naval power in the Philippines within the first crucial days of the war, the Japanese gained supremacy that isolated the Philippines from reinforcement and resupply. The Philippines also provided airfields for support of Japanese invasion forces and staging operations in the South Pacific.

Allied survivors of the devastating Japanese attacks on the Philippines fought valiantly as infantry but were no match for the well-equipped enemy. They were forced to surrender and were subjected to the Bataan Death March. Lieutenant Newman took part in that march; he was initially listed as a prisoner of the Japanese on May 7, 1942, before his death was confirmed later that year on August 13th. His body was not recovered and his name was listed on the monument at Fort William McKinley in Manila, the Philippines. Lieutenant Newman is also honored on the World War II Memorial at Santa Barbara High School.

Virginia described Bob as the "*most wonderful and handsome brother that any family could have! He was so kind and good, more than any of us can imagine….. No son and brother could have been loved more [than] he was."*

When the National World War II Memorial Registry of Remembrances was established in conjunction with the World War II Memorial in Washington DC in 2004, Virginia honored her beloved brother as one who had served in the Philippines from 1941-43, then taken prisoner and finally died on the Bataan Death March. Virginia still has the lovely handkerchief he sent her one year for Christmas.

The *Santa Barbara News Press*, May 30, 1943

LIEUTENANT RICHARD OESCHLER, JR.

Lt. Richard Oeschler, Jr.

Richard was the only child of Richard, Sr. and Elsie Oeschler. Richard Senior was a German immigrant who came to Santa Barbara to work for the Fred S. Tucker Company as an interior decorator. In 1924 he opened his own shop on State Street. He soon outgrew the space and moved his business to larger quarters at the corner of State and Carrillo Streets in downtown Santa Barbara. He made drapes, upholstered furniture, and offered decorating advice for many residents of Santa Barbara and Montecito.

Young Richard attended local schools and graduated from Santa Barbara High School in 1938 where he had been a member of the Scholarship Society and on the varsity tennis team. He then attended Santa Barbara College before transferring to the University of Hawaii. He was also employed by the Southern Counties Gas Company.

On April 21, 1942, Richard enlisted in the Army Air Corps at the Santa Maria Air Field and took his initial training at Santa Ana. By November, he was attending the bombardier school in Roswell, New Mexico. On Christmas Day Richard married Gretchen Hirt in the post chapel at Roswell. Gretchen was also a graduate of Santa Barbara High School and, perhaps not so coincidentally, she was the daughter of an upholsterer. Gretchen was a stenographer at the time of their marriage.

In January 1943 Richard completed his flight training in bombing and aerial tactics. He was commissioned as a second lieutenant and received his bombardier wings. He went on to navigator school in Alexandria, Louisiana, and was promoted to first lieutenant. Originally the Army planned to train men for the dual positions of bombardier and navigator. Richard was in the second class to receive the dual training. He joined the 444th Bombardment Group as a member of the 677th Bomber Squadron.

The 444th was the first B-29 Superfortress combat group established. It entered combat in the Pacific Theater in June 1944 and was considered an elite unit as only the top 10% of Air Corps recruits, technicians, mechanics, pilots, and aircrew were selected to take part in this B-29 program.

The B-29 Superfortress, similar to the one Lt. Richard Oeschler, Jr. was assigned as a navigator

Lieutenant Oeschler was assigned to the Dudhkundi Air Field in India. The airfield was originally designed for B-24 Liberator use. In 1943, it was re-designated as a B-29 Superfortress Base for the planned deployment to India of the Army Air Force XX Command. It was one of four B-29 bases established by the Americans in India and was upgraded to Superfortress operations using thousands of Indian laborers.

The 444th was part of the Operation Matterhorn project of the XX Bomber Command whose purpose was to bomb the Japanese home islands. In order to reach Japan, the B-29s needed to stage operations from Kwanghan Air Field, a base in south-central China. All the supplies of fuel, bombs, and spare parts needed to support Kwanghan had to be flown 1200 miles from India over "The Hump" (the name given by Allied pilots to the eastern end of the Himalayan Mountains) since the Japanese controlled the seas around the Chinese coast. For their role, the B-29s flying in these supplies had to be stripped of nearly all combat equipment and used as flying tankers. Each carried seven tons of fuel for the six hour flight. "The Hump" was so dangerous and difficult that each time a B-29 flew from India to China, it counted as a combat mission.

On November 11, 1944, Lieutenant Oeschler was the navigator on a B-29. Its target was Omura, Japan. Before reaching Japan, the aircraft developed an oil leak in one of its engines and the pilot left the formation. The airplane was heard trying to contact a submarine for about fifteen minutes. Another aircraft sighted the plane ditched in the water just off Shanghai near a river. Photographs of the downed plane were taken from 19,000 feet which showed the plane afloat with a large oil slick surrounding it. Apparently no life rafts were spotted and white spots on the plane's wing may have been some members of the crew. Two Japanese single engine aircraft were seen in the immediate vicinity.

Major Herman F. Smith had been an eyewitness to the downed plane. In February 1945 he was interviewed and described what he saw:

> "The plane had made a crash landing off the east coast of China in the East China Sea. The plane had made a crash landing and the entire crew was seen sitting on the wing of the plane waving for help. They could not pick them up because the planes cannot land on the sea. That was the last they were seen or heard of."

Richard apparently lost his life that day and his body was never recovered. He is memorialized on a monument at Fort William McKinley in Manilla, the Philippines, and was awarded the Purple Heart and the Air Medal.

Flier Missing On China Mission

One of the first Santa Barbara fliers to hold the distinction of becoming a bombardier and navigator, Lieutenant Richard John Oeschler, Jr., has been reported missing in action.

The information was sent to his wife, Gretchen Hirt Oeschler, who revealed Tuesday that the flier was reported missing in China. The last time he had been home was in June.

According to the War department telegram, the lieutenant has been missing since Nov. 9. Ironically enough, in the last letter to his wife, written just two days before he disappeared, Oeschler said he was getting along well and had just gone over the "hump," the mountain barrier between China and India. Mrs. Oeschler expressed the belief that her husband probably was lost in one of the B-29 raids as he had been flying in that type of craft before he left the States.

Lieutenant Oeschler is the son of Richard J. Oeschler and Mrs. Elsie Oeschler. He joined the service in April, 1942, and received his commission and first wings in January and was classed as a bombardier. In March he graduated as a navigator and was awarded a second pair of wings.

Santa Barbara News Press, November 28, 1944

Richard and Gretchen had a daughter Kathleen who was born in January of 1944. After Richard's death, his father had a home built for Gretchen and her little girl on Hot Springs Road in Montecito. Gretchen remarried when Kathleen (who went by Kathy) was six years old; Kathy was raised by her mother and stepfather, Homer Lloyd Hendrix. Kathy's younger sister Melinda was born in 1953.

Radioman Second Class William Thomas Owens

William Owens was the oldest of three children born to Myrick and Anne Thomas Owens in Carbon, Indiana. Myrick operated a grocery store in the small town of West Terre Haute, Indiana. In December 1920, he married Anne Thomas. Two years later William (known as Bill) was born.

William Owens graduated from Santa Barbara High School in 1940

By 1934, the family had moved to Santa Barbara and lived on De la Vina Street. Myrick was the branch manager of the Great A&P Tea Company, a position he held until he and Anne moved to Fontana about 1944. While in Santa Barbara, the family moved several times before settling for several years at 179 Hope Avenue.

Bill attended local schools including Santa Barbara High School where he graduated with the Class of 1940. In late December 1941, he enlisted in the Naval Reserve and was sent to Los Angeles for his initial training. He became an aviation radioman, second class, and was called to active duty. He was assigned to the VT-11, a torpedo squadron in the Pacific.

Second Class William Owens

The VT-11 Torpedo Squadron was commissioned in October 1942. The pilots flew the Grumman TBF/TBM Avenger, a carrier-based torpedo bomber affectionately known as *The Turkey*. The squadron was land-based from January 1943 until mid-summer 1944. The planes operated from Kanton Island, Guadalcanal, Pearl Harbor, and Fiji Island. The assignments during this time period included anti-submarine defense, search and rescue, patrol missions, strikes, and setting mines.

On June 8, 1943, Bill was one of ten passengers on an R4D-F, a Marine Corps transport plane that had taken off at night from Tontouta Air Field, New Caledonia, with a crew of fourteen. These planes provided transportation services in the South Pacific. Just after takeoff, one of the transport's engines failed and the pilot, First Lieutenant Neal G. Williams, attempted to turn back. The plane stalled and crashed into St. Vincent's Bay. All personnel were lost including Aviation Radioman (ARM) W.T. Owens.

Santa Barbara's Fallen Aviators of World War II

William T. Owens was remembered on the Tablets of the Missing at the National Memorial Cemetery of the Pacific, Honolulu, Hawaii. His brother Robert honored him in 2004 on the National World War II Memorial Registry of Remembrances established in conjunction with the World War II Memorial in Washington DC. He is also honored on the World War II Memorial at Santa Barbara High School.

National Memorial Cemetery of the Pacific, Honolulu, Hawaii

LIEUTENANT CLIFFORD JOSEPH PECK
(This tribute was written by David J. Peck, the aviator's nephew)

Lt. Clifford Joseph Peck

Clifford J. Peck was born in Santa Barbara on September 4, 1918, the third child and second son of Edgar L. Peck and Bertha S. Peck. He attended Garfield Elementary School, La Cumbre Junior High, and graduated from Santa Barbara High School in 1938.

Clifford learned to fly as a teenaged civilian at the Santa Barbara Airport, flying a small Aeronca. He entered the service to his country in the US Army Air Corps in the late 1930s, and was trained as an aircraft mechanic and "propeller specialist." He held the rank of sergeant by the time of Pearl Harbor on December 7, 1941.

After Pearl Harbor and with America needing many new pilots, Clifford applied for and was accepted into cadet pilot training. He received his "wings" and graduated from Advanced Army Air Force Flying School on August 6, 1942 at Craig Field, Alabama (birthdate of his nephew Len Peck, Jr., a native of Santa Barbara). His advanced flight training was taken exclusively in the Bell P-39 "Airacobra."

Second Lt. Peck was assigned to the 111th Observation Squadron, (later renamed the 111th Tactical Reconnaissance Squadron) at Fort Dix, New Jersey, in 1942. He shipped out with other US soldiers/airmen on the *Queen Mary* in October 1942, arriving in Scotland later that year.

On January 15, 1943, Clifford flew with other members of his squadron from Portsreath, England, to Port Lyautey as part of the deployment of the 12th Air Force that was activated in support of the Allied invasion of North Africa. The squadron flew from England nonstop to Morocco in their P-39s, with several of the squadron members' "low gas" warning lights flashing red upon touchdown in North Africa. For the next several months the squadron flew in support of the invasion of North Africa, flying reconnaissance missions in Algeria, some anti-submarine patrols in the Mediterranean, and reconnaisance missions around the Spanish Moroccan border. Many of the pilots in the squadron only had a few hundred hours of flight time by the time they reached North Africa.

During March 1943, the fabled German "Afrika Corps," under the command of General Erwin Rommel, successfully attacked the American line at Kasserine Pass in Tunisia and created great havoc among the American army. Clifford was temporarily assigned to the 154th Reconnaisance Squadron during this battle, flying several combat missions in southern Tunisia. This is his diary entry for March 15, 1943:

> "We flew south past Gafsa, hit the deck over the lake to the southeast of Gafsa, and passed over American trucks....A truck and sedan were southwest of the pass in the second range. We came through the pass and started to get shot at. Tracers were going by me to the left and in front of me. Several men

> were behind the gun. I turned left and let them have a short burst. I think I got them, but wasn't sure as I passed over so quickly. Then I saw a truck in a ravine in front of me and gave it a short burst. I hit it but didn't see it catch on fire."

Clifford's squadron was among the first American squadrons to obtain the new P-51A "Mustang" in North Africa. This model of the famed plane was much different to fly than the tricycle landing geared P-39, and several pilots, including Clifford "nosed" the tail-dragging P-51A when landing, damaging the propellers. There was apparently no official instruction in learning how to fly these new planes. The P-51s were delivered to the pilots and they were expected to learn how to fly them with a minimal amount of instruction.

After the defeat of the Italians and Germans in Tunisia in May 1943, the Allies turned their attention to their next stop, Sicily. The invasion, code-named *Operation Husky*, began on July 10, 1943. Clifford's initial sorties were flown in the P-51 from Korba, Tunisia, into southern Sicily, but the squadron transferred to the newly captured Ponte Olivo airport in southern Sicily on July 14. Using the P-39s for the first time during the Sicilian invasion, Clifford took off for a reconnaissance mission of the area around Agrigento, where American troops were pushing inland against the German/Italian forces. The official 111th TRS diary stated that date:

> "Using our P-39s for the first time on a mission for the new campaign we lost our first pilot 1st Lt. Peck. He failed to come back from a low level recon mission near Agrigento. No word from him at all and it is believed he crashed somewhere in enemy territory."

On July 18, the squadron historian wrote in the record,

> "Still no word about Lt. Peck. Been missing for forty-eight now so missing in action report was turned in."

And on July 24, 1943,

> "Telephone call brought word that Lt. Peck's plane and body had been found and that he was buried in American Cemetery near Licata on the 20th of the month. No explanation of the crash could be found."

In research I did on my late uncle Clifford, I contacted former members of his squadron who reported that they had been told that Clifford was mistakenly strafing American ground troops and was shot down by American ground fire near Agrigento, Sicily, the morning of July 15, 1943. Some of the members of the 111th searched for and discovered Clifford's crash site near Agrigento and took photos of it that they supplied to me in 1990.

Clifford Peck was awarded the Purple Heart and Air Medal. His squadron was awarded the French Croix de Guerre for their remarkable service during WWII in North Africa, Sicily, Italy, France, and Germany.

Calvary Cemetery
Santa Barbara, California

LIEUTENANT JACK PERES

Jack Peres was born to John and Louise Buch Peres in Santa Barbara on March 5, 1920. His father was a Kansas native who moved to California permanently with his parents and siblings about 1906. His mother was a Polish immigrant who came to the United States in 1903. John had various occupations – he was a machinist, auto mechanic, and truck driver. When the couple was first married, they lived in Santa Barbara; then in the mid-1920s they moved with their two children to Fillmore. John operated the Ford dealership there for several years. They came back to Santa Barbara in the mid-1930s and the children attended Santa Barbara schools.

Jack Peres graduated from Santa Barbara High School in 1937

Jack was a graduate of Santa Barbara High School Class of 1937. While a student, he had been a member of the Scholarship Society, the varsity tennis team, and ROTC as a sergeant. After high school Jack attended Santa Barbara College, then UCLA where he studied medicine with the goal of becoming an army surgeon. He enlisted on New Year's Eve 1940 at March Field in Riverside as an aviation cadet. He was commissioned a second lieutenant at Kelly Air Field and then in early 1942 was assigned as a pursuit pilot of the 33rd Pursuit Squadron (Provisional), 8th Pursuit Group of the Far East Air Force. His squadron was based in Australia.

The P-40 fighter plane, the type of aircraft flown by Lt. Jack Peres

During Jack's training, his family moved to Burbank where they took jobs at Lockheed Aircraft to support the war effort. Louise was a material sorter; Leona, Jack's sister, a transportation clerk; and John used his mechanical skills as a jig builder.

Sadly, Jack's career as a pursuit pilot was short lived as he was shot down over Darwin, Australia, on February 19, 1942. On that day, he and a squadron of ten pursuit planes were forced by unfavorable weather to turn back from a ferry flight from Darwin, Australia, to Koepang, Dutch Timor. When the flight arrived at Darwin and before the planes could refuel, the pilots engaged in a fierce battle with a Japanese force of 114 bombers and fighters. Three of the planes were shot down, including the one flown by Lieutenant Peres.

Six months later the body of Lieutenant Peres was found inside his P-40 fighter plane in the jungles of northern Australia. His plane was found pitted with bullet holes and it appeared that Peres had attempted to land his plane before he died.

Santa Barbara's Fallen Aviators of World War II

Distinguished Service Cross Awarded Lt. Peres, Air Hero

Headline from the *Santa Barbara News Press*, September 8, 1942

Just three days earlier, he had been posthumously awarded the Purple Heart and the Distinguished Service Cross for extraordinary heroism. The Service Cross citation stated in part,

> *"Lieutenant Peres, in spite of the tremendous odds, courageously attacked the enemy formation, inflicting heavy damage, and continued the attack until his airplane was shot down. Second Lieutenant Peres' unquestionable valor in aerial combat, at the cost of his life, is in keeping with the highest traditions of the military service and reflects great credit upon himself, the Far East Air Force, and the United States Army Air Forces."*

In September 1942 the lieutenant's parents and sister attended a subdued ceremony at Lockheed to receive Jack's medals. There was no elaborate ceremony, no long line of troops, and no review for the awarding of these medals. Instead at the request of his family, the presentation was held at lunch time so no production time at the defense plant would be lost.

Lieutenant Jack Peres and other former students who died during the war effort were honored in December 1942 at Santa Barbara College. A memorial flag in their honor was donated by a campus sorority and presented to the college president to be hung in the foyer of the administration building. Ten gold stars were also created to symbolize those ten men who had died that year and would never return to the campus. In 1948, the Santa Barbara City Council named one of the streets at the Santa Barbara Airport after Jack.

Jack's body was returned to Santa Barbara and buried in the Santa Barbara Cemetery where his grandfather Herman Peres had been buried a year earlier. Jack's parents were later laid to rest in this same cemetery.

Santa Barbara Cemetery, Santa Barbara, California

Local Aviator's Valor In Darwin Battle Is Cited

Posthumous award of the Distinguished Service Cross has been made to Lieutenant Jack Peres of Santa Barbara and three members of his squadron for heroism in carrying out an attack on a greatly superior force of enemy aircraft, it has been announced from General MacArthur's headquarters in Australia.

They lost their lives when their planes, part of a squadron of 10 American pursuit ships, were shot down near Darwin in February after dauntlessly giving battle to a force of 115 Japanese bombers and fighters.

LEADER HONORED

The men honored were: Major Floyd Pell, Ogden, Utah, squadron commander; Lieutenant Charles Hughes, Jr., Cincinnati; Lieutenant Elton Perry, Phoenix, and Lieutenant Peres.

The American squadron was returning to its base at Darwin from Kupang, on Dutch Timor, Feb. 19, when it unexpectedly came upon the huge Japanese formation which included 60 high-level bombers, 18 dive-bombers and 37 escorting fighters.

JAPS HIT HARD

The report sets forth that without thought of the odds, nearly four to one in fighters alone, the Americans dived to the attack and inflicted heavy damage on the enemy. They destroyed a number before their own ships were shot down into the sea.

Lieutenant Peres, 23, left his medical studies at the University of California to become a fighter pilot. His father, John A. Peres, and sister, Miss Leona Peres, are employed at Lockheed Aircraft, helping to build more planes for such heroic young men. The family formerly resided here. His grandmother, Mrs. M. L. Peres, and his aunt, Mrs. Ethel M. Clark, reside here.

Recently Mr. and Mrs. Peres were advised of the final action in which their son took part by Lieutenant-Colonel Charles H. Morehouse, aid-de-camp to General MacArthur, who expressed to them the general's sympathy and his desire "that you be assured that this sacrifice will not have been in vain, for ultimately victory will be ours."

***Santa Barbara News Press*, September 8, 1942**

MASTER SERGEANT JACK B. RICKARD

Jack was born April 7, 1920, to Roy F. and Irma Burleson Rickard. Both he and his older brother George were born in Santa Barbara. Roy and Irma separated when the boys were young; she managed an apartment house on Bath Street and Roy owned a farm in Goleta.

After his parents separated, Jack lived with his mother while George was cared for in an institution in Sonoma, California. Jack attended local schools and graduated from Santa Barbara High School with the Class of 1937. While in school he participated in several intramural sports including basketball and track. His goals after high school were to attend college and then own a ranch.

Jack Rickard, a 1937 graduate of Santa Barbara High School

Jack joined the Army about 1940 and took his training in aviation mechanics in Glendale, California. He was assigned to the 437th Bombardment Squadron of the 319th Bomber Group. The 319th began combat in November 1942 and was based on the coast of North Africa flying the B-26 Marauders. This aircraft gained a reputation as a widow maker due to the high rate of accidents during takeoff and landings of its early models.

However, after using more experienced pilots, the B-26 had the lowest combat loss rate of any US aircraft used during the war. By the end of World War II, it had flown more than 110,000 sorties and had dropped 150,000 tons of bombs; it had been used in combat by British, Free French, and South African forces in addition to US units. In 1945 when B-26 production was halted, 5,266 had been built.

During the Second World War, the North Africa Campaign took place from June 10, 1940, to May 16, 1943. It included campaigns fought in the Libyan and Egyptian deserts and in Morocco, Algeria, and Tunisia. Early on, the job of the 319th was to attack airdromes, harbors, rail facilities, and other targets in Tunisia. It also struck at enemy shipping to prevent supplies and reinforcements from reaching the enemy in North Africa.

Goleta Soldier Killed In North Africa Area

A telegram from the adjutant general in Washington, D. C., informed Roy Rickard of Goleta that his only son, Jack B., master sergeant in the Army Air forces was killed in the North African area.

"The Secretary of War asks that I assure you," the message said, "of his deep sympathy in the loss of your son Master Sergeant Jack B. Rickard. Report just received states that he died April 17, 1943, in North Africa area as a result of airplane accident. Letter follows."

Sergeant Rickard had been in the Army over three years. Prior to joining the service he worked with his father on the latter's Goleta ranch. He was a graduate of the Santa Barbara High school and took his aviation mechanic's training at Glendale.

Santa Barbara News Press, May 5, 1943

Santa Barbara's Fallen Aviators of World War II

From March 3 to April 25, 1943, the 319th Bombardment Group was based at Oujda Air Field in the Oriental Region of Morocco near the Algerian border. Jack Rickard was killed on Saturday, April 17, 1943. He had attained the rank of master sergeant before his death.

His death was the result of an airplane accident but the circumstances surrounding the mishap are yet to be revealed. Master Sergeant Rickard is buried in the North Africa American Cemetery in Carthage, Tunisia, along with First Lieutenant John H. Minter, a fellow crew member.

Sgt. Jack B. Rickard was buried in the North Africa American Cemetery, in Carthage, Tunisia

LIEUTENANT KENNETH E. ROBERTS

Kenneth was born on August 7, 1922, the second child of Phillip and Sara Menning Roberts. At the time the family was living in Pasadena, California, where Phillip sold cars. By 1930, Phillip and Sara had moved with their three children to Santa Barbara and were living a short distance from the Santa Barbara Mission on Paseo del Descanso. In Santa Barbara, Phillip was employed as a stock broker and later became the manager of the local Dean Witter office.

Lt. Kenneth E. Roberts

Kenneth and his sisters attended local schools, graduating from Santa Barbara High School. Kenneth was in the Class of 1940. During his high school days, he was editor of The Forge, the school's newspaper, and a member of the Scholarship Society. Kenneth hoped to be a writer after attending college. According to his school chum, Bob Carlson, he was a good student and went on to attend the University of California, Berkeley.

He interrupted his junior year to join the Army Air Force and enlisted as a private in the Army Reserves out of Lincoln, Nebraska, on March 4, 1943. He began flight training in Santa Ana in June and continued training at the University of Idaho and Santa Maria's Hancock Field. He earned his pilot's wings as a fighter pilot at Luke Field in Arizona on February 8, 1944, and was commissioned as a second lieutenant. He was sent on to Baton Rouge, Louisiana, for further assignment.

The P-47 Thunderbolt, the model of aircraft flown by Lt. Kenneth Roberts

His prowess as a P-47 Thunderbolt pilot sent him to Europe as part of the 389th Fighter Squadron, 366th Fighter Group. The P-47 gradually became the Army Air Force's best fighter-bomber. It could reach speeds of 433 mph, climb to 43,000 feet, and had a range of 800 miles in combat. It could carry two 500-pound bombs, eight machine guns, and ten unguided rockets. Between June 6, 1944, and May 7, 1945 (VE Day), the Thunderbolts destroyed 86,000 railroad cars, 9,000 locomotives, 6,000 armored fighting vehicles, and 68,000 trucks.

Lieutenant Roberts was stationed in Normandy along the French coast and served as a pursuit pilot. His job was to strafe German tanks behind the enemy lines. It was a dangerous job as the squadron lost over 70% of its pilots. Lieutenant Roberts died August 2, 1944, less than six months after earning his wings.

The following day, First Lieutenant Lawrence G. Charbonneau gave this account of the accident:

> "I was leading Slipshod White flight with Lieutenant Roberts as my wingman, Lieutenant Phillips flying White 3 and Lieutenant

Morgan White 4. We were flying in a broken line astern formation at 3000 feet under a 6/10's overcast, visibility ¾'s to 1 ½ miles.

We were looking over a wooded area at St. Sever Calvados when heavy 20mm flak was observed to be coming from these woods. Spotting a heavy gun position in the woods, Lieutenant Morgan and I dropped our bombs on it, scoring hits. Lieutenant Roberts in the meantime was circling overhead on my instructions. I rejoined the flight at about 3000 feet and, at that time, Lieutenant Roberts called out that he was hit. Flak was very intense. Calling to him, I told him to jettison his last bursts of flak which followed from the main flak concentration area.

After these last hits were seen, his plane slow rolled to the left and lost about 1500 feet altitude. The plane seemed to level out at about seven hundred feet, as if the pilot was trying to bring it under control. The plane continued on in a dive of about thirty degrees and exploded when it hit the ground at approximate coordinate T-536495. The pilot was not seen to leave the plane, nor did the bombs seem to explode."

Lt. K. E. Roberts Killed at Front

On the day his parents, Mr. and Mrs. Philip Roberts, 16 West Los Olivos street, received word that he was missing in action, Second Lieutenant Kenneth E. Roberts, U. S. Army Air Forces, was killed close behind the Normandy front lines.

The United States government so informed Mr. and Mrs. Roberts in a telegram Tuesday.

Lieutenant Roberts gave his life for his country Aug. 2, while serving in his capacity as a pursuit pilot strafing tanks behind the German lines.

The 21-year-old officer interrupted his junior year at the University of California to join the Air Forces on March 1, 1943. He graduated in 1940 from Santa Barbara High school, where he edited the school paper.

During his training period in the service, Lieutenant Roberts was stationed at Lincoln, Neb.; the University of Idaho; Santa Ana Army Air Base, and Hancock Field and Tucson. After graduation from Luke Field, Ariz., he was sent to Harding Field, Baton Rouge, La., and from there to England and France.

His mother has been sponsor of the Co-Eddettes since their organization before Pearl Harbor.

Santa Barbara News Press, September 21, 1944

For his heroism, Lieutenant Roberts was awarded the Purple Heart. In 2004, he was honored by his sister Mary Ellen Knappe on the National World War II Memorial Registry of Remembrances established in conjunction with the World War II Memorial in Washington DC. In 1948, the City of Santa Barbara named the streets of the Santa Barbara Airport for local aviators who lost their lives during World War II. A street at the airport bears Kenneth's name.

Kenneth Roberts was buried in the American Saint Laurent Cemetery, the precursor to the present-day Normandy American Cemetery. It was the first American World War II cemetery on European soil and was established just two months before Ken's death. Today it contains the graves of 9,387 of our military dead.

SERGEANT CLARENCE ROBERT SAWYER, JR.

Clarence Robert Sawyer, Jr. was born in 1912 in California to Clarence Robert and Carrie Phelps Sawyer. Though he was named for his father, the aviator went by his middle name, Robert.

Clarence Sawyer, Jr.

Clarence Senior emigrated as a child from Canada and his family settled in Carpinteria. Carrie was a Wisconsin native. Like his father, Clarence was a farmer, and he and Carrie raised their three children in Carpinteria.

Robert first attended Santa Barbara High School where he was president of his class, then moved on to Carpinteria High School where he was vice-president of the student body and editor of the Carpinteria High School yearbook. He graduated with the Class of 1929. He attended Santa Barbara College and completed three years of college at UC Berkeley before returning home.

In Carpinteria Robert took up farming, perhaps working for his father. Clarence and Carrie lived on Linden Avenue and Robert lived next door. He married Virginia Fennell and continued to live on Linden Avenue when their son Robert Fennell was born in May 1935.

On March 29, 1944, at the age of 32, Robert enlisted as an Army private out of San Pedro. He was trained as a gunner on a B-29 and assigned to the 29th Bombardment Group, 6th Bombardment Squadron. His squadron was sent overseas and based in Guam in February 1945. The 29th flew sixty-six combat missions. The targets varied from airfields, aircraft factories, chemical plants, oil refineries, and industrial areas.

A photograph from the 1929 yearbook of Carpinteria High School with Sawyer in top row, far right

The first mission was to Tokyo on February 25, 1944, and the last one was on August 15. By now, General Curtis LeMay was in charge of the raids over Japan. His goal was to destroy those industries which supported the Japanese war effort. To achieve his goal, he initiated night raids because the Japanese night fighter forces were relatively weak. The initial raids were successful and, in April, General LeMay ordered attacks on the aircraft engine factories at Musashi and Nagoya and on the urban areas of Tokyo, Nagoya, Osaka, Kawasaki, Kobe, and Yokohama.

One of those attacks began early on April 7, when 153 B-29s struck the aircraft-engine complex at Nagoya, destroying about ninety percent of that facility though at a loss of American lives. Robert had just been promoted to sergeant when his plane, piloted by

Santa Barbara's Fallen Aviators of World War II

William Buttfield, took off. Just after 2:00 a.m. on April 7, the plane with a crew of eleven and one passenger was hit by enemy anti-aircraft fire over Nagoya. The strike caused the left wing of the plane to shear off and the plane went into a flat tail spin and crashed. All on board were killed.

Though successful in destroying much of the Japanese war machine, the cost to the 29th Bombardment Group was enormous. Eighteen crews, including the Buttfield crew, were lost over the six months of raids.

On October 8, 1993, the Air Force Academy honored the 29th Bombardment Group with a special ceremony at the dedication of a Memory Wall. The Academy's honor roll included Sergeant Clarence R. Sawyer, Top Gunner, United States Army Air Force.

Along with nine of his fellow crew members, Clarence Robert Sawyer is listed on a grave marker at the Jefferson Barracks National Cemetery in St. Louis, Missouri. He is also remembered on the Carpinteria High School World War II Memorial.

Clarence Senior died in 1961 and Carrie in 1972. Both are buried in the Carpinteria Cemetery. Virginia Sawyer remarried in 1962 and passed away in 1990.

Cpl. Sawyer Listed Missing

His B-29 bomber destroyed over Nagoya when the left wing was torn off by Jap flak April 7, Cpl. Clarence R. Sawyer, husband of Mrs. Virginia Sawyer, 10 Las Encinas Rd., has been listed missing in action by the War Department. Other airmen on the raid reported that a number of unidentified fliers were seen to leave the bomber by parachute, according to information Mrs. Sawyer has received from her husband's commanding officer. The couple have a son, Robert, 10.

Cpl. Sawyer is the son of Mr. and Mrs. C. R. Sawyer of Carpinteria. He attended Santa Barbara and Carpinteria Union High Schools, Santa Barbara College, and the University of California at Berkeley. He has been in the service since March, 1944, and overseas since February. Cpl. Sawyer was a fire control gunner on the B-29.

Other Tri-County casualties listed Wednesday were:

Pvt. Leland Lewis, husband of Mrs. Luceal M. Lewis, Rt. 1, Fillmore, wounded, Pacific Area.

Pfc. Ignacio R. Flores, son of Mrs. Jesus R. Flores, 462 N. Garfield Ave., Oxnard, wounded, European Theater.

Pvt. Inasio C. Tovias, USMCR, husband of Mrs. Inasio C. Tovias, 312 S. Ojai St., Santa Paula, wounded, Pacific Area.

Santa Barbara News Press, June 6, 1945

Along with nine of his fellow crew members, Clarence Robert Sawyer is listed on a grave marker at the Jefferson Barracks National Cemetery in St. Louis, Missouri

SERGEANT STANLEY HOWARD SOTO

Three brothers, one war. Stanley (Stan) Howard Soto was born on September 25, 1919. He was the third son of Peter J. and Susan J. Soto. He and his brothers, Bernard and Francis, were born in San Luis Obispo where their father owned a grocery store. The family later moved to Santa Barbara where their parents divorced.

Their father married Josie and the boys lived with them on Voluntario Street. Later the family moved to Ashley Road and Peter worked as a gardener in Montecito. They later moved back into Santa Barbara where Peter worked at various jobs including driving a truck.

Stanley H. Soto

Stan and his brothers attended Santa Barbara High. While there, Stan was active in sports playing football, basketball, and baseball and running track. He was a member of the Student Legislature during his junior and senior years. Like many young people, Stan hadn't decided his future plans when he graduated in 1937.

As young adults, the boys lived with their mom, first on East Anapamu Street, and then on Chapala Street. Before they all entered the service, Bernard worked in a bakery and later as a salesman for TR Welch, and Francis was employed by The Town House, first as a clerk, then as a bartender. Stanley worked for an auto detail shop owned by George Young. None married before enlisting.

Bernard and Stan were the first to enlist. Bernard joined the Army July 18, 1940. He volunteered to serve in the Signal Corps as part of the Philippines Campaign. He became a staff sergeant before he was captured by the Japanese in May 1942. Sergeant Bernard Soto died in a Japanese prison camp in the Philippines on December 6, 1942.

That same year, Stan joined the Marine Corps and attended boot camp in San Diego. In December 1942, he graduated from the Marine Corps parachute trooper school near Santee (San Diego County) after six weeks of training. Francis enlisted in the Army out of Fresno the following April.

Stan saw two tours of duty as a Marine, the first in the Pacific for eleven months as a paratrooper. Then, in early 1945, he was sent to Iwo Jima to join the Fifth Marine Division. The Fifth was never considered a "green" outfit, even from the very start. It counted among its ranks thousands of combat veterans, many of them, like Sergeant Soto, former members of various paratroop companies.

SGT. STANLEY SOTO
Killed on Iwo Jima

Stanley Soto Killed In Action

Sergeant Stanley Soto of Santa Barbara has been killed in action on Iwo Jima, his mother, Mrs. Sue Soto, 516 West Canon Perdido street, was informed by the Marine Corps commanding general on Friday. His father, P. J. Soto, lives here at 324 West Carrillo street. The telegram announcing his death said it took place on March 2.

Less than a month ago Mrs. Soto had received a letter from her son telling of the invasion and subsequent battles on Iwo. He called the rocky, volcanic island "Purple Heart Isle" and told how his platoon spearheaded the drive to the top of Mount Surbachi.

En route to the invasion of Iwo, he had met his brother, Corporal Francis Soto, on Bougainville, he told his mother in the letter. Another brother, Sergeant Bernard Soto, was taken prisoner by the Japs when Bataan fell and subsequently was reported to have died in a prison camp in the Philippines.

Santa Barbara News Press,
March 31, 1945

Santa Barbara's Fallen Aviators of World War II

On February 19, 1945, the Fifth Marine Division and the Vth Marine Amphibious Corps assaulted Iwo Jima where they were met with fierce fighting, clawing their way forward a yard at a time. Across Motoyama Airfield #1, up Mount Suribachi, and then onto the Motoyama Plateau, the Fifth fought and died. Foot by foot, day by day, the Marines pushed forward until the Japanese were finally crushed on March 25th. It was here they earned their nickname, *The Spearhead*.

Shortly after he arrived on Iwo Jima, Stan wrote in a letter to his mother:

> *"No doubt you know that I am at Iwo Jima and that our battalion secured Mount Surabachi. It was a wonderful sight and a glorious feeling to see Old Glory flying from the top of the mountain.*
>
> *Our company did a wonderful job and I can honestly say our platoon was outstanding. We spearheaded the drive to the mount and my squad was on the front all the way. I am sure proud of these boys. We had only one casualty, and that wasn't serious.*
>
> *They ought to call this place Purple Heart Isle, as we sure caught hell. This is a souvenir hunter's paradise, but I haven't gotten any yet and I don't want any."*

He ended his letter by telling his mother,

> *"Don't worry, as I am being as careful as possible."*

2 Brothers Dead In War, 3rd Soto Given U.S. Duty

In consideration of family sacrifice and contribution to the war effort, Cpl. Francis P. Soto will be relieved from combat duty overseas and permanently assigned to the United States, the War Department has announced. He is the sole surviving son of Peter Soto, Carrillo Street, and Mrs. Sue J. Soto, 972 Church Street, San Luis Obispo.

The War Department's action was in accordance with a policy adopted by the Army whereby the sole surviving son of a family which has lost two or more sons in the service of their country shall be retained in or returned to the continental limits of the United States for permanent assignment.

The Soto family's two other sons were lost in war service. Sgt. Bernard J. Soto died while a prisoner of war. Sgt. Stanley H. Soto was killed in action last March 2 on Iwo Jima.

Cpl. Soto was born Oct. 13 1917, at San Luis Obispo. He was inducted April 7, 1943, at Fresno, and is a member of Company K, 182nd Infantry.

Santa Barbara News Press, May 13, 1945

Sadly Sergeant Stanley Soto had actually been killed on Iwo Jima, March 2, 1945, before his mother received the letter. She was informed of her son's death by a telegram sent by the Marine Corps commanding general on March 30.

Weeks earlier while en route to the invasion of Iwo Jima, Sergeant Soto had met his brother, Corporal Francis Soto, on Bougainville while Francis was on his way to the Philippines. Corporal Soto's assignment there was short lived. He was relieved from combat duty in May and permanently assigned stateside duties. A War Department policy had been put in place which stated that the sole surviving son of a family who had lost two or more sons in the service of their country could not serve overseas and would be assigned duties in the continental United States.

Staff Sergeant Bernard Soto was buried at Fort William McKinley, Manila. Sergeant Stanley Soto was buried in the National Memorial Cemetery of the Pacific in Honolulu. He was awarded the Bronze Star and Purple Heart. A street at the Santa Barbara Airport bears Stanley Soto's name honoring his service to his country.

WASP Trainee Betty Pauline Stine

Betty was a 1939 graduate of Santa Barbara High School

Betty loved flying, as did her great uncle Will Rogers. The petite, brown-eyed girl planned to become an airline stewardess after her graduation from Santa Barbara High School. Instead she joined the Women Airforce Service Pilots (WASP) and became a pilot in her own right.

Betty was born September 13, 1922, in Fort Worth, Texas, the only child of Jake and Mary Allen Stine. She was named for her great-aunt, the wife of famed humorist Will Rogers. The family moved to Goleta in 1930 and Jake worked in the grocery business. Later he was a truck driver, then a dehydrator operator for Pacific Western Oil Company. He also travelled the rodeo circuit as a calf-roper riding Cowboy, a favorite horse that once belonged to his uncle Will Rogers. Perhaps it was Jake's free-wheeling spirit that inspired Betty to reach for the clouds.

Betty attended Santa Barbara High School and graduated in 1939. She took a job in a local retail store while attending Santa Barbara College and still living at home. She then enrolled at the University of Arizona when the aviation bug bit her. Meantime, Betty's mother operated a beauty shop on State Street while the family resided on the upper eastside on Anacapa Street.

In 1943, at age 21, Betty was accepted into the Women's Air Ferrying Service. She began her training at Avenger Field in Sweetwater, Texas, in September as part of Class 44-W-2. It would be her responsibility to ferry planes from the factory to the airfields and from one airfield to another. Male pilots would be available for other military duties. She learned to fly the AT-6 "Texan", a member of the Advanced Trainers which first entered service in 1938.

In a letter to her mother, Betty's instructor wrote the following:

WASP Trainee Betty Pauline Stine

> "Betty is the best girl pilot I have ever had the pleasure of knowing and her coordination (which is essential in flying) is flawless. She has her heart in her flying and does not resent criticism, which I might say is an attribute, because most girls resent criticism, whether constructive or otherwise. It doesn't matter to Betty whether the air is rough or smooth. She flies equally well in both elements."

Unfortunately, Betty was never able to test her prowess while serving in the military. While she was completing her training as a WASP, she was on a cross-country training flight along with thirteen other female pilots. They had departed Sweetwater and landed in Blythe on Thursday, February 24, 1944, to spend the night. The next morning on her return to Sweetwater, Betty's plane developed engine trouble soon after take-off. She parachuted from her plane and landed in rugged mountain country near Tucson, Arizona. Strong winds dragged her body over sharp rocks and, though she was found alive that afternoon, she died later in the evening from her injuries. Her parents had already arrived in Texas to attend the ceremony where Betty would receive her wings.

Miss Stine was given a full military funeral and granted her wings and uniform posthumously. In 2004 she was honored by both Ralph Bozorth and the WASP WWII Women on the National World War II Memorial Registry of Remembrances established in conjunction with the World War II Memorial in Washington DC. Only a year earlier, the Women Airforce Service Pilots were finally honored and recognized for their contribution to the war effort.

Betty Stine was one of thirty-eight WASPs who died while serving her country. Betty and her parents are buried in the Santa Barbara Cemetery.

Santa Barbara Cemetery, Santa Barbara, California

Miss Betty Stine, 22, Killed In Air Crash

Miss Betty Stine, 22, daughter of Mr. and Mrs. Jake Stine, 2231 Castillo street, was fatally injured late Friday afternoon in an airplane crash near Blythe, her aunt, Mrs. Glen Frazee, 1089 Ontare road, was informed Friday night.

Miss Stine was in training as a Wasp and was on a cross-country training flight when she was killed, Mrs. Frazee said. Mr. and Mrs. Stine are in Fort Worth, Tex., visiting relatives and had planned to be at Sweetwater, Tex., when their daughter received her wings next week. They are expected to return here over the weekend.

Mrs. Frazee said she called the operations officer at the Blythe Army Air Field Saturday morning and he told her Miss Stine's plane was one of 14 on the cross-country flight. They had arrived at Blythe Thursday evening, had stayed overnight and were starting their return flight to Sweetwater When Miss Stine's plane developed trouble about 20 miles out of the field.

The young aviatrix parachuted from her plane, other members of the formation reported, and her parachute was seen to open satisfactorily. She landed in rugged mountain country and searching parties found her still alive about 4:30 p.m. She died at 10 o'clock Friday night. No other details were released pending a military inquiry.

Blythe Field officials said the body probably would not be released for funeral services here for at least two days.

Santa Barbara News Press, February 26, 1944

LIEUTENANT GEORGE PARKER TOMS, JR.

George Parker Toms was named for his father but was always known as Parker. He was born in New Jersey July 10, 1921, the second child of George and Marion Fagan Toms. He had a sister born in 1919 (who died soon after) and four younger siblings. His family did not live year-round in the Santa Barbara area but they did have a beach house in Sandyland (just west of Carpinteria), and Parker did marry a local girl.

George P. Toms, Jr.

His lineage is rather interesting as he was the grandson of an Irish immigrant. His maternal grandfather, Lawrence Fagan, rose from an ironworker in New Jersey to chief executive of an ironworks manufacturing plant and mayor of Hoboken, New Jersey (1894-1901). His paternal grandmother, Bessie Parker, was a Washington DC mover and shaker, especially in Republican circles, and quite a community activist in support of the American presence during World War I.

Parker's father was a successful financier who moved his young family to the West Coast, first settling in Pasadena then moving north to the Bay Area. It was quite a shock when he died at the young age of forty-four. His obituary noted that he "played an important part in both the depression and recovery period of coast banking and finance." He was also a crusader. He and four other wealthy Bay Area men brought an unsuccessful suit against the state of California to test the constitutionality of the state's income tax law enacted in 1935. Besides being a banker, he also sat on several corporate boards. As a young man, he was awarded the Croix de Guerre from the French government for his demonstrated bravery during World War I.

Lt. George P. Toms, Jr.

George Parker and Marion had married in 1918 in New York and raised five children. Marion was a strong, independent woman in her own right and worked diligently to keep the family fortune intact.

Parker Toms attended the prestigious Lawrenceville Preparatory School in New Jersey and completed his education in 1940. He was enrolled at the University of California before he enlisted in the military. In September 1941 he joined the Royal Air Force and trained in Canada as part of the Eagle Squadrons. These fighter squadrons were formed during World War II with volunteer pilots from the United States and operated within the Royal Air Force (RAF) Command. The basic requirements for those interested in joining the Eagles were a high school diploma, ages between twenty and thirty-one, and good eyesight. The recruits also had to show 300 hours of certified flying time.

In the March 13, 1942, edition of the *Los Angeles Times*, an announcement appeared stating that Jacqueline Schmitz and Parker Toms Jr. had married in Toronto, Canada, on March 4. The news came as great surprise to family and friends. Jacqueline, a year younger than Parker, had lived in the Bay Area and also in Carpinteria.

Parker was sent off to England in May where he spent several weeks learning to fly various aircraft before being posted to a squadron. Then he was sent to Atcham Airfield near Shropshire, home to the 6th Fighter Wing of the Eighth United States Army Air Force.

Initially Atcham was used as an operational fighter base. Then, beginning in late 1942 when the field was transferred to the United States, its primary use was one of operational training for fighter pilots for both the Eighth and Ninth Army Air Force Units.

Parker was assigned to the 495th Fighter Training Group which flew Spitfires and Bell P-39 Airacobras. He had attained the rank of second lieutenant. While based in England,

Atcham Airfield, near Shropshire, England, was Lt. Toms's assigned station at the time of his death

his daughter Wendy was born on Christmas Day 1942 in Santa Barbara. Less than three weeks later, Lieutenant Toms was killed in a flying accident over Roden (near Atcham Airfield) when his Spitfire experienced engine failure.

It wasn't until December 1948 that Parker's body was returned by ship to New York, then sent on to the West Coast for burial in Golden Gate Cemetery in San Francisco.

Lt. George P. Toms, Jr. is buried in Golden Gate Cemetery San Francisco, California

Corporal John Robert Troup

Corporal John Robert Troup

John and his twin sister, Jeannie Elizabeth, were born in Santa Barbara on May 14, 1917, two and a half years after their big brother, William Gordon. Their parents were John and Jeannie Main Troup and the family lived on the Ripley Ranch at the north end of San Marcos Road. Growing up, the three children were known as Gordon, Bobby, and Betty.

A happy childhood eluded the Troup children. Their father died of a ruptured appendix when the twins were ten years old. Three years later they were orphaned when their mother took her life. Gordon went out on his own and Betty and Bobby moved to Fillmore to live with an aunt and uncle. When Bobby was sixteen, he was sent off to Cal Poly to finish his education. There he took courses in agriculture and, at age eighteen, he found work on a ranch in the San Francisco area. From there, he returned to Santa Barbara to work as a herdsman at the Dos Pueblos Ranch.

After the war broke out, Bobby (now known as Bob) enlisted in the Marines. He was still single while his twin sister was married and living in Goleta. Bob trained at Camp Pendleton as a navigator before being assigned to the 279th Platoon. While in training in San Diego, he won medals in sharpshooting and pistol firing. This Scottish family thought it was fitting that their Bob was sent to defend New Caledonia, a Pacific island whose name translated to New Scotland!

Along with French Polynesia and the New Hebrides, New Caledonia was part of the French South Pacific colonies which joined the Free French Forces. These colonies became vital Allied bases in the Pacific Theater. The United States built a major naval base on New Caledonia to combat the advance of the Japanese toward Australia, New Zealand, and the Solomon Islands. If left unchecked, Japanese advances threatened to sever the sea lanes between North America and Australia.

Bob Troup First Goletan Killed In War Zone

Corp. John Robert Troup, U. S. Marine Corps, has died in action in the South Pacific, to be listed as Goleta's first known casualty of the war.

Word of his death, in a plane crash, was received here Wednesday night by his grandfather, John Troup.

Bob, as he was known to his many friends, was 25 years of age and had been in service about seven months. He was born in Goleta and was employed as cattle foreman on the Wylie ranch at Dos Pueblos.

Beside his grandfather he is survived by his maternal grandmother, Mrs. Robert Main, his twin sister, Mrs. Norman Rowe, and a brother, William Gordon Troup, all of Goleta. Both his parents are dead.

His loss is doubly felt as he was looked upon as the logical successor to his grandfather — one of the nation's most noted livestock judges. Bob had been a student at California Polytechnic in San Luis Obispo.

Goleta Valley Leader,
October 16, 1942

Corporal John R. Troup and his crew were killed on New Caledonia October 9, 1942, while transporting fuel. Their overloaded plane crashed into a mountain on takeoff. Betty remembers getting the news of her brother's death while working at the walnut house near the railroad tracks in Goleta.

John Robert (Bob) Troup and Norman Firestone (another aviator) were among the first Santa Barbara casualties of World War II. In honor of their service, they were lain in state at the Santa Barbara County Courthouse. Bob is buried in the Goleta Cemetery alongside his parents, with his four grandparents laid to rest nearby.

Goleta Cemetery, Goleta, California

Goletan Honored Posthumously

(The following story was written by Technical Sergeant Jim G. Lucas, U.S. Marine corps, Tulsa, Okla., and distributed by the Associated Press).

SOMEWHERE IN THE SOUTH PACIFIC, June 4 (Delayed)—Corporal John Robert Troup of Goleta has been praised posthumously by his commanding officer for his part in keeping open an aerial supply route to Henderson field during the battle for the Solomon Islands.

Corporal Troup was killed when his plane crashed near the mouth of the Lunga river, Guadalcanal, last Nov. 13.

RISKED HIS LIFE

Repeatedly, Corporal Troup risked his life to ride as navigator on Navy cargo transport planes loaded with bombs, high explosives and gasoline into Guadalcanal, helped to unload under fire on Henderson field's bomb-battered runways, and then took off into hostile skies for the return trip with a load of battle-wounded marines for base hospitals out the fighting zone. Against Japanese attack, his plane was defenseless save for the skill of its pilot.

Corporal Troup enlisted March 4, 1942 at Los Angeles and joined his command within a few months.

Colonel P. K. Smith, commander of a Marine Air group in the South Pacific, praised Corporal Troup "for outstanding heroism in the line of his profession while serving as flight navigator of naval transport aircraft while operating in the Solomon Islands area," and set out:

TEXT OF STATEMENT

"During the period of Sept. 1 to Oct. 9, 1942, Corporal Troup made seven trips as flight navigator of Navy cargo transport aircraft in the Solomon Islands area.

"His zeal, exceptional courage and devotion to duty during these flights, under extremely hazardous conditions, enabled this group to supply combatant forces and evacuate wounded

Santa Barbara News Press, June 27, 1943

LIEUTENANT EDWARD GEORGE VERHELLE

Children born to George and Angela Carteri Verhelle in Santa Barbara were Yvonne, Irma, and Edward (Eddie), who was born on Easter Sunday, March 27, 1921. Before attending junior high and high school, the children attended a private school run by Mrs. Eichler. The family lived on E. Micheltorena Street near the site of the former St. Francis Hospital and attended Our Lady of Sorrows Church in downtown Santa Barbara.

The Santa Barbara High School yearbook described Eddie, saying,

Lt. Edward G. Verhelle

> *"It is either the soldier in his blood or the long hours of study and practice that made Ed a success in ROTC. From a private, he rose to the ranks of Sergeant Major, First Lieutenant, and Captain. In addition to all of this, he was battalion adjutant and a member of the Hearst Trophy Rifle Team."*

After he graduated in 1939, he attended Santa Barbara College but enlisted before finishing his education.

Irma remembers her brother as a prankster who loved to tease his sisters. He didn't have a specific girlfriend but was popular with lots of the girls! He loved to sail, especially star boats, and he crewed for a local dentist. They would enter boat races together in Newport Beach. Eddie also loved to fly so he joined the United States Naval Reserve as an aviation cadet. His father was greatly disappointed that he did not want to go into the family nursery business.

According to Irma, Edward actually enlisted twice – once in Pensacola, Florida, and the second time in 1942 with the Navy in Corpus Christi, Texas. He was appointed a Naval aviator on October 21, 1942, and was assigned to a Navy air squadron based in San Diego. The following year as a lieutenant he was put aboard an aircraft carrier headed for the Pacific. He once said, *"The biggest thrill is found not in bombing operations but in the return to the carrier and seeing the same number of planes that went out come back one by one."*

Edward was part of the Hellcat Squadrons based on the USS *Hornet* where he was dubbed "Blackie" by his fellow crewmen. His squadron saw duty over Tarawa, Truk, and the Marshall and Gilbert Islands.

In an undated letter, Eddie described his flying activities:

> *"We were on hand for the invasion of Iwo Jima, giving the ground forces close air support from the twentieth to the twenty-third of February. All of us got a first hand view of Mount Surabachi, which is to be on the posters for the sixth war loan. It was not so rough for us in the air, but the Marines had a pretty tough time there on that three by five mile island.*

Santa Barbara's Fallen Aviators of World War II

> *"We were to hit Kanoya on the nineteenth but we received word that most of the remaining Japanese Fleet was in the harbor at Kure Naval Base. Naturally, we being navy to the core, we are primarily interested in placing the enemy fleet in their half of the ocean. So we went after the ships.*
>
> *"Naturally all of us of the air group are proud to have been a part of this mighty force which stalked the enemy in his own habitat. Moreover we are happy to have been able to participate in what may well be the beginning of the end for our enemy in the Pacific."*

Lieutenant (j.g.) Verhelle was injured in the course of combat and was hospitalized for a time in Pearl Harbor. While convalescing, he met up with his friend Bill O'Brien from Santa Barbara who was a corpsman in charge of the lieutenant's ward. They enjoyed reminiscing about old times in Santa Barbara. After he mended, Eddie was sent back to his ship where he resumed his duties. On May 24, 1945, Lieutenant Verhelle was killed. He was on a fighter sweep over an enemy-held island. His job was to destroy installations on an airfield when, on his first strafing run, his plane was hit by enemy anti-aircraft fire and crashed. He was unable to bail out of the stricken plane.

Lieutenant Verhelle was awarded the Air Medal, the Gold Star, the Asiatic-Pacific Area Campaign Medal, a Purple Heart, the Distinguished Flying Cross, and a World War II Victory Medal posthumously. The citation accompanying the Gold Star and signed by the Secretary of the Navy read as follows:

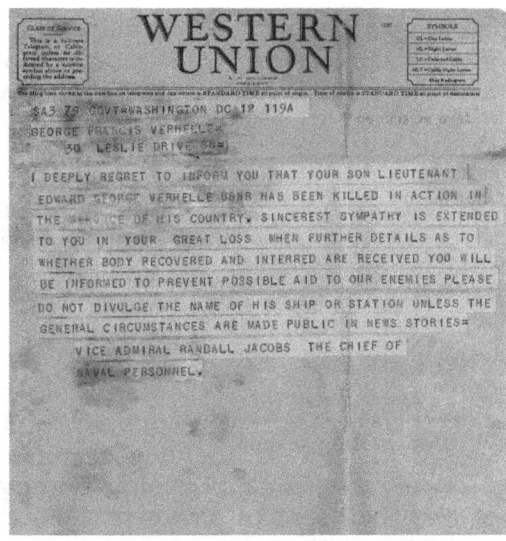

Telegram, dated June 12, 1945, informing Lt. Edward Verhelle's parents of this death

> "For meritorious achievement in aerial flight as Pilot of a Fighter Plane in Fighting Squadron SEVENTEEN, attached to the U.S.S. HORNET, during operations against enemy Japanese forces over the Tokyo area of Japan, Iwo Jima, Chichi Jima and Okinawa Shima from February 16 to March 1, 1945. Determinedly performing his duties, Lieutenant Verhelle pressed home his attacks and contributed greatly to the success of the assigned missions. His airmanship, courage and devotion to duty were in keeping with the highest traditions of the United States Naval Service."

During World War II, the USS *Hornet* was under heavy attack fifty-nine times but was never hit. The ship was damaged only when the hangar deck was torn apart by a typhoon. The ship also took part in the Korean and Vietnam Wars and finished its career by recovering the astronauts from Apollo 11 and 12. In 1995 the USS *Hornet* was designated a National Historic Landmark and saved from the scrap heap by a group of volunteers. Today it is docked at Pier 3 in Alameda, California, and is a floating museum.

On March 24, 1948, veterans' organizations of Santa Barbara selected Edward Verhelle to be honored with a street named for him at the Santa Barbara Airport. He is also remembered on the memorial at Elings Park and the National Memorial Cemetery of the Pacific, Honolulu, Hawaii.

CORPORAL ALAN LAVERNE WADE

Alan and his twin brother, Martin Peter Junior, were born November 16, 1923, in Santa Barbara. They were the only children of Martin and Matilda (Molly) Altenburg Wade. Martin Senior was a local rancher and Molly worked as a saleswoman for a Santa Barbara clothing store. The family lived on Mountain Drive, though they also owned property near Arroyo Burro (Hendry's) Beach known as Braemar Ranch. Interestingly, there are two streets nearby known as Wade Court and Alan Road, perhaps named for the family.

Alan L. Wade, a 1941 graduate of Santa Barbara High School

Both Alan and Martin attended local schools and graduated from Santa Barbara High School in 1941. While there, both boys were members of ROTC. They went on to enroll in the Brown Military Academy at Pacific Beach near San Diego. In the fall of 1942, Martin married Marianne Tenney while enrolled at Brown.

Alan enlisted the following February as a private in the US Army. He completed a 20-week course at the Technical School held at the Army Air Forces Training Command in Sioux Falls, South Dakota. He was then sent to Air Corps Gunnery School at Yuma, Arizona, where he achieved the rank of corporal. His final training was in Lemoore, California, where he was classified as a radio operator-gunner on a B-17 Flying Fortress. Martin, Alan's twin, also joined the service and trained as a radio operator-mechanic at Sioux Falls.

The Wade family was very proud of these servicemen. The Santa Barbara News-Press ran several news stories about the boys when they were able to come back to Santa Barbara for a visit. One such story appeared in the August 15, 1943, edition with the headline *Barbecue Fetes Wade Boy On Furlough*. Here is an excerpt:

"*In honor of their twin sons, Mr. and Mrs. M.P. Wade threw two barbecues, since both boys, servicemen in the army, couldn't get home at the same time on their furloughs.*

"*The later event was given in honor of Sergeant Martin Wade who came home last from Camp Wolters, Tex. at about the same time that his brother, Corporal Alan Wade, was on his way back to training quarters at Camp McCain, Miss. The parents gave the barbecue at the Braemer Ranch.*"

Then on August 14, 1944, the newspaper ran one more story, a sorrowful one. It reported the death of Alan Wade. He never saw combat but served his country just the same. He was killed in a plane crash near Walla Walla, Washington, on September 12, 1944.

CORP. ALLEN WADE
Victim of Plane Tragedy

Corporal Wade Dies In Crash

Corporal Allan Wade, 20, son of Mr. and Mrs. Martin Wade, 1525 Mountain avenue, was killed in the crash of an Army plane late Tuesday night, his parents were informed by long-distance telephone Wednesday. The crash occurred near Walla Walla, Wash. No details of the tragedy, which took the lives of the entire crew, were revealed.

The corporal, twin brother of Staff Sergeant Martin P. Wade, stationed at Fort Bliss, Tex., had been in the service since February, 1943. Before he joined the service, he was a student in a military academy in San Diego.

Funeral services are pending arrival of the body from the north.

Santa Barbara News Press, September 14, 1944

Alan is buried at the Santa Barbara Cemetery. He is honored on the World War II Memorial at Santa Barbara High School.

At the time of Alan's death, Martin was stationed in Fort Bliss, Texas. After the war, Martin and his wife settled in the Sacramento area where Martin died in 1976. Martin is buried in the cemetery alongside his twin brother and their parents.

Santa Barbara Cemetery, Santa Barbara, California

LIEUTENANT DEAN KENT WILBER

Dean K. Wilber, a 1938 graduate of Santa Barbara High School

Dean Wilber was a Santa Barbara native born to James and Cornelia Kent Wilber on May 24, 1920. His parents were from Ohio and had moved to California by the time Dean's sister Ruth was born in 1914.

Dean attended local schools and, while at Santa Barbara High School, participated in the ROTC program. He was a member of the Scholarship Society for three years and qualified to be a Seal Bearer in his senior year. Dean graduated from Santa Barbara High in January 1938 and took jobs in the composing room and the circulation department of the Santa Barbara News-Press. He then went to work for a local department store. He and Sylvia C. Day married in December 1939. They became the parents of two children, Glenn and Deanna.

On August 29, 1942, Dean enlisted. He began training at Camp Roberts and in November, already a corporal, he was selected to attend the Field Artillery Officers' Candidate School in Fort Sill, Oklahoma. He was assigned to the 12th Armored Division and took advanced training in piloting the "grasshopper" observation plane. These light aircraft carried no armaments; instead they were used for field and artillery spotting and directing artillery fire, and for light transport and courier services. Their ability to land and take off from small, primitive landing strips made them ideal front-line aircraft.

Upon graduation from officers' training in February 1943, Corporal Wilber was commissioned a second lieutenant and sent to a liaison flight school at Pittsburg, Kansas. He received his liaison flight wings July 1944. After a short time at Camp Gruber, Oklahoma, Dean was assigned to the 250th Field Artillery Group headquartered in France. During the Battle of the Ruhr Pocket, he served as an aerial forward observer. This battle took place in late March and early April 1945, and was, for all intents and purposes, the final dagger in Nazi Germany's war effort. More than 300,000 of their troops were taken as prisoners as Allied troops encircled the Ruhr area of Germany.

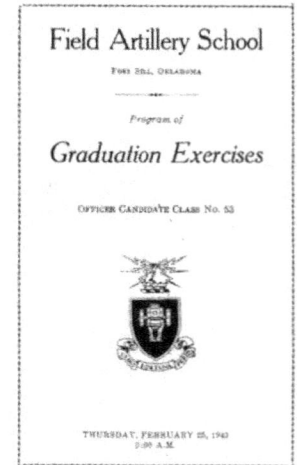

The program of Lt. Dean Wilber's graduation from Officer Candidate School

The German armed forces officially surrendered on May 8, 1945, and Lieutenant Wilber remained in Europe. He was first stationed in Cologne, Germany, and then served for three months in Heilbronne. What took him on to France remains unknown; he was killed in a plane crash there on September 1, 1945. He had achieved the rank of first lieutenant prior to his death.

Santa Barbara's Fallen Aviators of World War II

Lieutenant Wilber was buried in the Lorraine American Cemetery in St. Avold (Moselle), France, and later honored by his son, Glenn, in 2004 on the National World War II Memorial Registry of Remembrances established when the World War II Memorial was dedicated in Washington DC.

Sylvia Wilber remarried. She and her husband, John Rennie, raised her two children and their son John. Sylvia passed away October 13th, 2003, in Templeton, California.

Santa Barbara News Press,
September 18, 1945

Private Sam M. Yee

Sam Yee was born in 1909 in the Cantonese village of Toysan in China. When and why he came to California is unknown though he did leave a wife and son behind in China. Sam completed only one year of high school but he worked for many years as a steward for the Santa Barbara Club on Chapala Street where he also lived.

He enlisted in the Army from Santa Barbara on May 5, 1942. It was not unusual for Chinese men to join the Armed Services. In fact, when Congress repealed the Exclusion Act in 1943, many Chinese men enlisted as a way to receive their citizenship. About one quarter of the Chinese-American military served with the Army Air Forces, including Private Yee. Like Yee, about forty percent of the Chinese-American soldiers were not native-born citizens.

United States Army Air Forces insignia

There is no record of where Private Yee trained or what skills he acquired. The circumstances leading to his disappearance and death were initially listed as missing in action; his death was later confirmed as occurring on February 3, 1943. He had been one of 904 servicemen on a transport ship, the USAT *Dorchester*, bound for Greenland when it was struck by a torpedo from a German U-Boat. The ship had been built as the SS *Dorchester* in 1926 for the Merchants and Miners Transportation Company to carry passengers along the East Coast between Boston and Miami. Following America's entry into World War II, the ship was brought out of mothballs, converted to a troopship, and entered into Army service in February 1942. It carried troops from Staten Island to Greenland military bases and back.

**Tablets of the Missing
East Coast Memorial
New York, New York**

After the February 3 attack, only 299 passengers survived the blast and the frigid Atlantic waters. Private Sam Yee died that day and his body was never recovered. He was awarded the Purple Heart and his name is listed on the Tablets of the Missing on the East Coast Memorial in New York City.

This memorial commemorates those soldiers, sailors, marines, coast guardsmen, merchant marines, and airmen who met their death in the western waters of the Atlantic Ocean during World War II. Its axis is oriented on the Statue of Liberty. On each side of the axis are four gray granite pylons upon which are inscribed the name, rank, organization, and state of each of the 4,609 missing in the waters of the Atlantic. This is Private Yee's inscription:

Sam M. Yee Private US Army Air Forces

Army Air Corps California

BIBLIOGRAPHY

(Note: The family information for each aviator came from records found in the public domain unless otherwise noted)

ADAMS, CLYDE MCALLISTER
U.S. World War II Army Enlistment Records, 1938-1946. http://www.ancestry.com.
Santa Barbara News-Press, "3 County Casualties Reported," May 4, 1943.
Ventura County Star Free Press, "Former Venturan Killed in Airplane Crash," May 8, 1943.
U.S. Army Air Force. Restricted War Department Report of Aircraft Accident, (revised May 15, 1943).
Santa Barbara News-Press, "Funeral Rites Set For Clyde Adams, Killed in Plane Crash," May 16, 1943.
Santa Barbara Cemetery Interment Records.
P-38 Lightning. http://www.wikipedia.org.
National Archives & Records Administration. War Department files. http://www.archives.gov.

ARNOLD, DEAN ALDEN
Olive & Gold, Santa Barbara High School yearbook, 1938.
U.S. World War II Army Enlistment Records, 1938-1946. http://www.ancestry.com.
Santa Barbara News-Press, "From the Fronts," September 13, 1942.
U.S. Army Air Force, 1941-1948. War Department, Missing Air Crew Report #12972, March 11, 1945. http://www.footnote.com.
Santa Barbara News-Press, "One Local Man Missing, Second Reported Dead," April 5, 1945.
Erwin, Sgt. Henry M, "History of the 29th Bomb Group," April 19, 1945. http://www. 29bg.com.
U.S. Rosters of World War II Dead, 1930-1945. http://www.ancestry.com.
"Firebombing (Germany and Japan) Air Attack on Tokyo." http://www.pbs.org/the war.
Santa Barbara News-Press, "College Alumni Who Gave Lives To Be Honored," June 2, 1943.
Jefferson Barracks National Cemetery, St. Louis, Missouri.

BATES, PHILIP HENRY
Eric Swensumson (aviator's nephew), correspondence and photos.
Santa Barbara News-Press, "Third Brother Joins United States Forces," May 31, 1941.
Santa Barbara News-Press, "Carpinterian Dies in Crash," July 13, 1942.
Trenton Evening Times, "Jersey Cadet Is Killed in Crash of Plane," July 14, 1942.
Santa Barbara News-Press, "Carpinteria Pilot Rites Monday," July 15, 1942.

Santa Barbara News-Press, "College Alumni Who Gave Lives To Be Honored," June 2, 1943.
Carpinteria Cemetery Interments.

BECKNELL, WALLACE EARL
Herman Becknell (aviator's brother), photos and phone interview, August 7, 2009.
U.S. World War II Army Enlistment Records, 1938-1946. http://www.ancestry.com.
U.S. WWII Military Personnel Missing in Action or Lost at Sea, 1941-1946. http://www.ancestry.com.
World War II and Korean Conflict Veterans Interred Overseas. http://www.ancestry.com.
U.S. Army Air Force. War Department Missing Air Crew Report #2238, February 5, 1944. http://www.footnote.com.
Santa Barbara News-Press, "One Local Man Missing, Second Reported Dead," April 5, 1945.
Lensink, Wendy, "Wallace Earl Becknell Lost at Sea," 303rd Bomb Group, (accessed July 27, 2009). http://www.ancestry.com.
Warren Stafford Jr. American Battle Monuments Commission, the World War II Honor Roll.
List of War Graves of U.S. Airmen in the Netherlands. http://www.airwarweb.net/margraten.

BOTELLO, FRANCIS L.
Phillips, Michael James. "Maclovio A. Botello," *History of Santa Barbara County.* Chicago: The S.J. Clarke Publishing Company,1927.
U.S. World War II Army Enlistment Records, 1938-1946. http://www.ancestry.com.
Santa Barbara News-Press, "Army Graduates Francis Botello," September 19, 1942.
Office of the Commanding Officer, Headquarters 745th Bombardment Squadron (H), May 6,1944.
U.S. Army Air Force. War Department Missing Air Crew Report # 4749, May 10, 1944. http://www.footnote.com.
Santa Barbara News-Press, "Ploesti Oil Fields Heavily Attacked," May 18, 1944.
Santa Barbara News-Press, "Sergeant Botello Lost in Romania," May 25, 1944.
Globalsecurity.org/space/facility/buckley, "Buckley AFB," (accessed November 20, 2009).
U.S. Veterans Gravesites, ca. 1775-2006. http://www.ancestry.com.
U.S. Rosters of the World War II Dead. http://www.ancestry.com.
Francis L. Botello Gravesite, Jefferson Barracks National Cemetery.

BURNS, JAMES EDWARD
Mary Ellen DuBois (aviator's wife); Bill DuBois (Mary Ellen's son); and Katy Lamb (daughter of Mary Ellen and James Burns), correspondence, July, August 2009.
U.S. World War II Army Enlistment Records, 1938-1946. http://www.ancestry.com.
Santa Barbara News-Press, "Mrs. J.E. Burns, Jr. Joins Husband in Sioux City," May 7, 1944.
Santa Barbara News-Press, "Lieutenant and Mrs. J.E. Burns Parents of Girl," May 12, 1944.
U.S. Army Air Force. War Department Missing Air Crew Report #14282, April 14, 1945. http://www.footnote.com.
Santa Barbara News-Press "Burns, Commander of Santa Barbara Superfort, Missing," May 20, 1945.

Santa Barbara News-Press, "Wife of Capt. Burns Receives DFC Award At Santa Maria Army Air Field Ceremony," July 31, 1945.
U.S. Rosters of World War II Dead, 1939-1945. http://www.ancestry.com.
U.S. Veterans Gravesites, ca. 1775-2006. http://www.ancestry.com.
World War II Honoree Killed in World War II. http://www.ancestry.com.
Memorandum for: Chief, Casualty Branch, Review and Determination of Status Under the Missing Persons Act, April 15, 1946.

CARMAN, EARNEST DARREL
Nevada State Journal, "Susanville Dramatists Give Play at Camp," March 24, 1937.
Reno Evening Gazette, "College Students Organize Club," September 13, 1938.
U.S. World War II Army Enlistment Records, 1938-1946. http://www.ancestry.com.
Santa Barbara News-Press, "Santa Barbaran at 65 Doing More Than A Bit," September 5, 1943.
U.S. Army Air Force. War Department Report of Aircraft Accident, May 20, 1944.
Santa Barbara News-Press, "Lt. Ernest Carmen (sic) Killed in European Air Battle," June 3, 1944.
Reno Evening Gazette, "Ernest Carmen (sic) Killed In Italy," June 9, 1944.
Nevada State Journal, "Pilot Killied (sic) in Italy Action," June 11, 1944.
Santa Barbara News-Press, "Local Woman Proud of 6 Service Stars, To Have Letter Read," December 17, 1944.
World War II and Korean Conflict Veterans Interred Overseas. http://www.ancestry.com.
U.S. Rosters of World War II Dead. http://www.ancestry.com.
World War II & Korean Casualty Listings. http://www.ancestry.com.
American Battle Monuments Commission, The World War II Honor Roll.
Combat Chronology of the US Army Air Forces (May 1944). http://www.usaaf.net.
Partain, Donald Frantz, "Unit History 'Gentlemen from Hell,' 487th BG, Station 137 Lavenham, England," *Bomber Legends*, no date.
Andrews, Roland and Peter Miller. "The Liberator Crash at Kentwell Hall, Long Melford." http://www.foxearth.org.uk/ww2Crashes.html.
487th Bombardment Group (Heavy) Group Markings. photo. http://www.487thbg.org/markings.html.
487th Bombardment Group. http://www.487thbg.org/photos.
487th Bombardment Group. http://www.mighty8thaf.preller.us.
Combat Chronology of the U.S. Army Air Forces, May 1944. http://www.USAFF.net.
Overseas American Cemeteries, Earnest T. Carmen, Cambridge American Cemetery, May 20, 1944. http://www.ancestry.com.

CASS, GERALD M.
U.S. World War II Army Enlistment Records, 1938-1946. http://www.ancestry.com.
Santa Barbara News-Press, "From the Fronts," November 1, 1942.
Santa Barbara News-Press, "Santa Barbara Airman is Pilot of Famous Bomber, 'Mary Lou,'" June 20, 1943.
Santa Barbara News-Press, "Local Flier Reported Air Medal Winner," February 17, 1944.
Santa Barbara News-Press, "Gerald M. Cass Believed Killed in Bomber Crash," February 17, 1944.
Santa Barbara News-Press, "Captain Cass Gets Oak Leaf Cluster," March 5, 1944.

U.S. Army Air Force. Missing Air Crew Reports of 1941-1948, Report #1380, May 11, 1944.
Santa Barbara News-Press, "Two Majors From Santa Barbara," July 2, 1944.
Fresno Bee Republican, "Fresno Major Is Lost On Biak Raid; His Men Honor Memory," September 21, 1944.
Santa Barbara News-Press, "Play Field Named For Gerald Cass," October 8, 1944.
Santa Barbara News-Press, "Widow to Receive Posthumous Award of Flier Husband," March 14, 1945.
Santa Barbara News-Press, "Mrs. Marie L. Cass Receives Air Medal," March 17, 1945.
World War II and Korean Conflict Veterans Interred Overseas. http://www.ancestry.com.

U.S. WWII Military Personnel Missing In Action or Lost At Sea, 1941-1946. http://www.ancestry.com.
"Randolph Air Force Base." http://www.wikipedia.org.
"Ruth Helen Cass Phillips." http://www.31stbombers.org/NEWSNOTES.htm.
5th Bomb Group Association website.

COOK, CECIL PALRANG, JR.
Olive & Gold, Santa Barbara High School yearbook, 1935.
U.S. World War II Army Enlistment Records, 1938-1946. http://www.ancestry.com.
Santa Barbara News-Press, "Sergeant Cook," September 26, 1943.
World War II Prisoners of War, 1941-1946. http://www.ancestry.com.
Santa Barbara News-Press, "Cecil Cook Lost In Prison Ship Sinking Off Mindanao Island," March 4, 1945.
Al Young Studios, "Personnel Lost At Sea As Result of Ship Sinkings During World War II," *My Father's Captivity,* 1998.
"World War II Prisoners of War Data File, 12/7/1941-11/19/1946, U.S. National Archives & Records Administration. http://www.archives.gov.
"Davao Penal Colony #502 (DEPOCOL)." http://www.mansell.com/pow.
"The *Shinyo Maru*: An Explosion, and Survival, for Some POWs," *American POWs on Japanese Ships Take a Voyage into Hell.* http://www.archives.gov/publications/prologue/2003/winter.
Mazza, Eugene A. "*USS Paddle: Sinking American POWs.*" http://www.microworks.net/pacific/personal/paddle.htm.
Shinyo Maru Hellship logo provided by *Shinyo Maru* Survivors Reunion, September 7, 1998.
World War II and Korean Conflict Veterans Interred Overseas. http://www.ancestry.com.
American Battle Monuments Commission, the World War II Honor Roll.
Manila American Cemetery and Memorial.
World War II Missing In Action or Buried At Sea. http://www.ancestry.com.

COURVILLE, EARL ALDEN
Olive & Gold, Santa Barbara High School yearbooks, 1939, 1940.
World War II Army Enlistment Records, 1938-1946. http://www.ancestry.com.
USAAF Stateside Accident Reports, Aviation Archaeological Investigation & Research (May 1943).
North Carolina State Board of Health, Certificate of Death, #22426, October 12, 1944.
Santa Barbara News-Press, "Car Crash Kills Pacific Veteran," October 13, 1944.
National Archives & Records Administration, War Department files, 2nd Lieutenant Earl A. Courville.

Santa Barbara's Fallen Aviators of World War II

COVERSTONE, ROBERT E.
Santa Barbara News-Press, "Coverstone Taking Bomber Pilot Course," May 11, 1943.
Santa Barbara News-Press, "From the Fronts," November 25, 1943; January 13, 1944; June 8, 1944.
The Salt Lake Tribune, "Society Today…Enid King, Grayce Elaine Martin, Brides-to-Be," April 20, 1944.
Oakland Tribune, "King-Coverstone Troth Plighted," June 24, 1944.
Battle Casualty Report, 305th Bombardment Group, October 23, 1944. http://www.footnote.com.
Santa Barbara News-Press, "Lieutenant Coverstone Is Killed In Action," November 14, 1944.
Virgil Coverstone (aviator's father). Correspondence between Virgil Coverstone and headquarters, Army Air Forces (1944-1945). http://www.footnote.com.
U.S. Rosters of World War II Dead, 1939-1945. http://www.ancestry.com.
World War II and Korean Conflict Veterans Interred Overseas. http://www.ancestry.com.
"2nd Lt John L. Touchett," forum. http://www.armyairforces.com.
World War II Honoree, Robert E. Coverstone, honored by Alexis Charles Witmer.
World War II Honoree, Robert E. Coverstone, honored by Marie B. Witmer.

DIBBLEE, FRANCIS RICHARD
Dibblee Hoyt (aviator's nephew), photos.
Santa Barbara News-Press, "Richard Dibblee…," June 1, 1943.
Santa Barbara News-Press, "In Northern California," January 31, 1944.
Santa Barbara News-Press, "Aviation Cadets Pietro (Peter) Dall'Armi and Francis Richard Dibblee…," May 29, 1944.
U.S. Army Air Force. War Department Missing Air Crew Report #14398, 98th Bombardment Squadron (H) May 19, 1945. http://www.footnote.com.
Santa Barbara News-Press, "2nd Lt. Richard Francis Dibblee Killed On Bombing Mission in Pacific War Theater," June 6, 1945.
Santa Barbara News-Press, "15 Tri-Countians on Casualty Lists," June 10, 1945.
World War II and Korean Conflict Veterans Interred Overseas. http://www.ancestry.com.
U.S. Rosters of World War II Dead, 1939-1945. http://www.ancestry.com.
U.S. WWII Military Personnel Missing In Action or Lost At Sea, 1941-1946. http://www.ancestry.com.
Air Corps Historical Records, 98th Bm. Sq. http://www.footnote.com.
B-24J Liberator Serial Number 44-40617. http://www.pacificwrecks.com.
National Archives & Records Administration, War Department file, 2nd Lieutenant Francis R. Dibblee.
World War II Honoree, Francis Dibblee, honored by Harold L. Vigue.

DONALDSON, JOHN LOUIS
Olive & Gold, Santa Barbara High School yearbook, 1940.
Wilda Donaldson Irvine (aviator's sister), interview and photos, July 22, 2009.
U.S. World War II Army Enlistment Records, 1938-1946. http://www.ancestry.com.
Santa Barbara News-Press, "Donaldson Prepares For Final Training," September 4, 1943.
Santa Barbara News-Press, "John Donaldson Commissioned," November 14, 1943.
Santa Barbara News-Press, "Donaldson Boys Write Home From England," July 4, 1944.
Santa Barbara News-Press, "Two Donaldson Boys Casualties," July 10, 1944.

U. S. Army Air Force Headquarters European Theater of Operations, Missing Air Crew Report # 06993, August 12, 1944. http://www.footnote.com.
2nd Lt. John L. Donaldson. http://www.100thbg.com.
World War II and Korean Conflict Veterans Interred Overseas. http://www.ancestry.com.
National Archives & Records Administration, War Department Records, 2nd Lieutenant John L. Donaldson. http://www.archives.gov.

ECKLES, REX ALBERT
Howard Eckles (aviator's brother), phone interview, August 2009.
Rex Lucas (son of Anthony Dean Lucas, a close war-time friend of aviator), correspondence.

Gwendolyn Waters (daughter of Anthony Dean Lucas, a close war-time friend of aviator), "Quest for B-17E 'Tokyo Taxi'," (updated October 29, 2009).
Olive & Gold, Santa Barbara High School yearbook, 1937.
U.S. World War II Army Enlistment Records, 1938-1946. http://www.ancestry.com.
Santa Barbara News-Press, "From the Fronts," July 5, 1942.
Santa Barbara News-Press, "6 Santa Barbara Soldiers Win Army Awards," July 14, 1943.
U.S. Army Air Forces. War Department Headquarters Missing Air Crew Report #10770, July 19, 1943.
Santa Barbara News-Press, "Lieutenant Rex Eckles Missing In Action," July 26, 1943.
Ventura County Star Free Press, "Somis Woman's Husband Missing," September 1, 1943.
Santa Barbara News-Press, "Eckles Missing, Says War Office," August 27, 1944.
Camarillo News, "Items About Folks You Know," September 8, 1944.
Santa Barbara News-Press, "War Record of College Shows Many In Service," November 5, 1945.
World War II and Korean Conflict Veterans Interred Overseas. http://www.ancestry.com.
PacificWrecks.com 1995-2011. http://www.info@pacificwrecks.org.
Rex A. Eckles, B-17 Pilot, 5th Bombardment Group, 23rd Bombardment Squadron. http://www.pacificwrecks.com.
American Battle Monuments Commission, the World War II Honor Roll, Tablets of the Missing at Manila American Cemetery, Manila, Philippines, Rex A. Eckles.

FIRESTONE, NORMAN SELWYN
Olive & Gold, Santa Barbara High School yearbook, 1938.
Santa Barbara News-Press, "From the Fronts," August 8, 1942.
Santa Barbara News-Press, "From the Fronts," February 9, 1943.
Santa Barbara News-Press, "Lt. Norman Firestone, Mustang Pilot, Missing In China," December 11, 1944.
Santa Barbara News-Press, "Battle Reports Add 12 To Tri-County List," December 17, 1944.
U. S. Army Air Force. Missing Air Crew Report #15648, India, Burma Theater December 23, 1944. http://www.footnote.com.
U.S. Rosters of World War II Dead, 1939-1945. http://www.ancestry.com.
74th Fighter Squadron. http://www.wikipedia.org.
23rd Fighter Group. http://www.globalsecurity.org.
Santa Barbara Cemetery interment.

FOWLER, JAMES LAURENCE

Olive & Gold, Santa Barbara High School yearbook, 1939.
Santa Barbara News-Press, "Navy Recruits 23 More Here," July 5, 1942.
Santa Barbara News-Press Photo caption, July 21, 1942.
Santa Barbara News-Press, "Lt. Fowler in Marine Squadron," May 23, 1943.
Santa Barbara News-Press, "Family Reunion Enjoyed by L.W. Fowlers," June 22, 1943.
Santa Barbara News-Press, "Lieutenant Fowler," June 24, 1943.
Santa Barbara News-Press, "Miss Nan Colt's Betrothal To Young Marine Flier Is Made Known To Friends," September 19, 1943.
Santa Barbara News-Press, "Nuptial Date Set Ahead At All Saints," October 17, 1943.
Santa Barbara News-Press, "Miss Frances Bacon Colt Becomes Bride Of Flier At Wedding At All Saints," October 24, 1943.

Santa Barbara News-Press, "Fowlers Return From Honeymoon in Carmel," October 31, 1943.
Santa Barbara News-Press, "Two Marine Lieutenants Get Advancements In Rank," January 1, 1944.
VTMB-233, Totokina Rabaul, 1st Lt. J.L. Fowler, February 14, 1944. http://www.aviationarcheology.com.
Santa Barbara News-Press, "Local Marine Flier Missing in Pacific," March 16, 1944.
Santa Barbara News-Press, "Missing Marine Flier Wins High Air Award," December 31, 1944.
Santa Barbara News-Press, "War Record of College Shows Many In Service," November 5, 1945.
World War II and Korean Conflict Veterans Interred Overseas. http://www.ancestry.com.
PacificWrecks.org 1995-2011. http://www.pacificwrecks.org.

GRIGGS, AUGUSTUS MONROE, JR.

Phillips, Michael James. "Augustus Monroe Griggs," *History of Santa Barbara County.* Chicago: The S.J. Clarke Publishing Company,1927.
Olive & Gold, Santa Barbara High School yearbook, 1941.
U.S. World War II Army Enlistment Records, 1938-1946. http://www.ancestry.com.
1943 Air Corps Grads Class WC 43-G, Personnel Records #28, from genforum, August 5, 2007. http://www.genealogy.com.
Santa Barbara News-Press, "Learning How," January 10, 1943.
Historic California Posts Santa Ana Army Air Base. http://www.militarymuseum.org.
Historic California Posts Ryan Airport. http://www.militarymuseum.org.
U.S. Army Air Force. War Department, Report of Aircraft Accident, August 14, 1943. http:www.aviationarcheology.com.
Santa Barbara News-Press, "'Gus' Griggs Air Accident Victim," August 17, 1943.
Santa Barbara Cemetery interments.

HARSHBARGER, WILLIAM MILLER

Dr. Kathy Corbera (aviator's niece), phone interview, August 24, 2009.
U.S. World War II Army Enlistment Records, 1938-1946. http://www.ancestry.com.
Santa Barbara News-Press, "From the Fronts," July 12, 1942.
Santa Barbara News-Press, "Anxiety Felt for Ex-Barbarenos Now Living in Hawaii, Philippines," December 8, 1941.
Santa Barbara News-Press, "Local Aviator Safe In Hawaii," December 12, 1941.
Santa Barbara News-Press, "Miss Sally Townsend's Troth To Hero of Solomons Battle Important News To Friends," May 30, 1943.

Santa Barbara News Press, "Miss Sally Park Townsend Becomes Bride of Hero Flier At All Saints-by-the-Sea," July 15, 1943.
Santa Barbara News-Press, "Harshbarger Given Awards," June 11, 1944.
U.S. Army Air Forces. War Department Report of Aircraft Accident, July 19, 1944. http://www.aviationarcheology.com.
Santa Barbara News-Press. "Captain Harshbarger Dies in Washington Crash," July 20, 1944.
Santa Barbara News-Press, "Harshbarger Rites Set For Tuesday," July 24, 1944.
The Reno-Gazette Journal, Obituary, Sally Knowles (aviator's wife), May 18, 2005.

HARTLEY, CYRIL OWEN
Olive & Gold, Santa Barbara High School yearbook, 1939.
Santa Barbara News-Press, "Hartley Enters Class of Cadets," December 27, 1941.
Santa Barbara News-Press, "Local Soldiers Get Promotions," January 13, 1942.
Santa Barbara News-Press, "Cyril Hartley Ends Basic Air Course," March 29, 1942.
Santa Barbara News-Press, "Flying Cadets In Training," April 23, 1942.
Santa Barbara News-Press, "Cyril Hartley Wins His Wings," October 11, 1942.
Vultee BT-13 Valiant. http://www.warbirdalley.com.
US Army Air Force. War Department Report of Aircraft Accident, Perrin Field, Sherman, Texas, May 15, 1943. http://www.aviationarcheology.com.
Santa Barbara News-Press, "Santa Barbaran Killed In Crash," May 16, 1943.
The Abilene Reporter-News, "Two Fliers Killed In Trainer Crash," May 16, 1943.
Santa Barbara News-Press, "Tri-County Men Who Have Given Lives in WWII Singled Out for Special 'In Memoriam'," May 30, 1943.
Santa Barbara News-Press, "College Alumni Who Gave Lives To Be Honored," June 2, 1943.
Santa Barbara News-Press, "War Record of College Shows Many In Service," November 5, 1945.
Santa Barbara Cemetery interment.

HAYS, JOHN WILLIAM
Frank Hays (aviator's brother), interview, September 3, 2009.
Keni Hays (aviator's son), photos and interview, September 3, 2009.
U.S. World War II Army Enlistment Records, 1938-1946. http://www.ancestry.com.
Camarillo Herald, "John W. Hays Dies in Action in Pacific," May 18, 1945.
Santa Barbara News-Press, "Pvt Hays Killed By Jap Sniper On Negros Island," May 27, 1945.
Santa Barbara News-Press, "4 Dead, 23 Wounded In Last Week's List," June 3, 1945.
503rd Infantry Regiment (United States). http://www.wikipedia.org.
U.S. Rosters of the World War II Dead. http://www.ancestry.com.
National Archives & Records Administration, War Department files, Pvt. John W. Hays
Santa Paula Cemetery interment.

HEBEL, FRANCIS FREDERICK
Mary Alice Coffman (aviator's niece), photos and interview, November 23, 2009.
Chismahoo, Carpinteria High School yearbook, 1929.
Alumni Review, "Alumni Called For Military Duty," by Captain F.S. Scott, California Institute of Technology, September 1941.
World War II U.S. Navy Aircraft Carrier Muster Rolls, 1939-1949. http://www.ancestry.com.
Los Angeles Times, "Toll Feared High in Attack Against Isles," December 8, 1941.

Santa Barbara News-Press, "Francis F. Hebel Of Carpinteria, Navy Flier, First War Casualty From County; Killed At Hawaii," (no date; in the collection of Mary Alice Coffman).

Santa Barbara News-Press, "Carpinteria Naval Officer First Local Casualty in New World War," December 19, 1941.

Santa Barbara News-Press, "Dies in Action," December 20, 1941.

Santa Barbara News-Press, "Hebel Memorial Service Today," December 28, 1941.

Journal of the Executive Proceedings of the Senate of the United States of America, Vol. LXXXIII, Seventy-Seventh Congress, first session from January 3, 1941 to January 2, 1942 with index (January 3, 1942). http://www.genealogybank.com.

Register of Commissioned and Warrant Officers of the U.S. Navy and Marine Corps, July 1, 1942, Serial Set Vol. # 10716, Session Vol. #37. http://www.genealogybank.com.

Santa Barbara News-Press, "Lieut. Hebel's Films To Be Exhibited," October 20, 1942.

Santa Barbara News-Press, "Lieut. Hebel's Films Carry His Service On," October 23, 1942.

Lundstrom, John B. *The First Team: Pacific Naval Air Combat from Pearl Harbor to Midway.*" Annapolis, Maryland. *Naval Institute Press,*1984.

"USS Enterprise CV-6, The Most Decorated Ship of the Second World War." http://www.cv6.org.

VF-6 Evening Strike Escort – 7 December 1941. http://www.cv6.org.

Hayes, Richard L. "Saga of Scouting Squadron 6." *Home & Garden Publications.* April 2004.

World War II Navy, Marine Corps, & Coast Guard Casualties. http://www.ancestry.com.

National Archives & Records Administration, War Department files.

Pearl Harbor Casualties. http://www.pearlharbor.org.

World War I, World War II, & Korean War Casualty Listings. http://www.ancestry.com.

U.S. Rosters of the World War II Dead. http://www.ancestry.com.

U.S. Veterans Gravesites, ca. 1775-2006. http://www.ancestry.com.

Overseas American Cemeteries, Honolulu, Hawaii.

KEISTER, ROBERT LOUIS

Enlisted Naval Aviation Pilots, USN, USMC, & USCG, 1916-1981, Robert L. Keister. http://www.bluejacket.com.

U.S. Marine Corps Muster Rolls, 1937, 1940. http://www.ancestry.com.

Santa Barbara News-Press, "Local Marine Earns Air Medal For Action," July 12, 1944.

US WWII Military Personnel Missing In Action or Lost At Sea, 1941-1946. http://www.ancestry.com.

Santa Barbara News-Press, "Four Marine Fliers Rip Jap Squadron In Split-Second Swoop," January 2, 1944.

Register of Commissioned and Warrant Officers of the United States Navy and Marine Corps (July 1, 1944).

Santa Barbara News-Press, "Missing Flier Wins Award For Heroism," July 2, 1944.

Service Personnel Not Recovered Following World War II, Defense Prisoner of War/Missing Personnel Office (DPMO). http://www.dtic.mil/dpmo/wwii.

National Archives & Records Administration, Navy Department files, 1st Lieutenant Robert L. Keister.

World War II and Korean Conflict Veterans Interred Overseas. http://www.ancestry.com.

State Summary of World War II Dead & Casualties California 1946. http://www.accessgenealogy.com.

Santa Barbara News-Press, "Posthumous, In Absentia Air Decorations Made," March 15, 1945.

LOPEZ, FREDERICK PETER
Olive & Gold, Santa Barbara High School yearbook, 1940.
U.S. World War II Army Enlistment Records, 1938-1946. http://www.ancestry.com.
Santa Barbara News-Press, "From the Fronts," December 3, 1942.
Santa Barbara News-Press, Navy Promotes James Lopez," November 21, 1943.
Santa Barbara News-Press, "Capt. F.P. Lopez Killed in Action," May 10, 1945.
Santa Barbara News-Press, "14 War Casualties Listed Last Week, May 13, 1945.
U.S. Rosters of the World War II Dead. http://www.ancestry.com.
World War II and Korean Conflict Veterans Interred Overseas. http://www.ancestry.com.
Overseas American Cemeteries, Lorraine American Cemetery, St. Avold, France.

National Archives & Records Administration, War Department files, 2nd Lt. Frederick P. Lopez.
Santa Barbara High School Alumni Newsletter (Fall, 2007).

LOVE, DAVID CULVER
George Love (aviator's brother), interview, August 3, 2009.
Olive & Gold, Santa Barbara High School yearbook, 1940.
Photo of David Love courtesy of http://www.b24.net.
Goleta Valley Leader, Untitled newspaper notice, February 20, 1942.
Santa Barbara News-Press, "From the Front," May 9, 1943.
Santa Barbara News-Press, "Marilee Stevens Engaged to Cadet Officer," December 15, 1943.
Santa Barbara News- Press, "Miss Marilee Stevens Becomes Bride of Lieutenant David Love," February 13, 1944.
Santa Barbara News-Press, "From the Fronts," June 29, 1944.
Crew Loading List for 7 July 1944. http://www.b24.net/missions.
Santa Barbara News-Press "Lt. David Love On Missing List," July 22, 1944.
U. S. Army Air Force. War Department, Missing Air Crew Report #07370, July 9, 1944.
Santa Barbara News-Press, "Hope Held For Safety Of Lieutenant Love," September 10, 1944.
Santa Barbara News-Press, "Missing Officer Reported Killed," October 31, 1944.
U.S. Rosters of the World War II Dead. http://www.ancestry.com.
World War II and Korean Conflict Veterans Interred Overseas. http://www.ancestry.com.
Santa Barbara News-Press, "Wife Receives Dead Husband's Citation," January 13, 1945.
Santa Barbara News-Press "Mrs. David Love Joins Parents For Summer," July 6, 1945.
National Archives & Records Administration, War Department files, 2nd Lt. David C. Love.
World War II Honoree, David Culver Love, honored by Mary H. Sonne, cousin.

MACFARLAND, ANDREW RANSALIER
Barbara Weissinger (aviator's wife), interview, August 5, 2009.
Andrew MacFarland (aviator's son), photos.
Olive & Gold, Santa Barbara High School yearbook, 1940.
U.S. World War II Army Enlistment Records, 1938-1946. http://www.ancestry.com.

Santa Barbara News-Press, "State College Romance Ends In Engagement," January 11, 1943.
Santa Barbara News-Press, "Barbara Chapman and Army Flier Marry at Mission," January 12, 1944.
B-24 Crew. http://www.picasaweb.google.com.
308th Armament Systems Group. http://www.wikipedia.org.
Santa Barbara News-Press, "Macfarland In Italian Base Hospital," May 7, 1944.
James E. Maher, Major Air Corps, signed letter, October 1, 1944.
Edward F. Mitchell, Major General, Adjutant General's Office, signed letter, October 12,1945.
Santa Barbara News-Press, "Lt. MacFarland Killed in China," October 14, 1944.
Santa Barbara News-Press, "Details of MacFarland's Death Told In Letter From Executive Officer," October 29, 1944.
U.S. Roster of World War II Dead. http://www.ancestry.com.

U.S. WWII Military Personnel Missing In Action or Lost At Sea, 1941-1946. http://www.ancestry.com.
World War II Honoree, Andrew MacFarland, honored by Mrs. Barbara Wessinger, wife.

MARXMILLER, ROBERT K.
Santa Barbara News-Press, "R.O.T.C. Cadets Will Visit Camp," May 2, 1941.
Santa Barbara News-Press, "Cadet Officers Hold Banquet," November 24, 1941.
Olive & Gold, Santa Barbara High School yearbook, 1942.
World War II Enlistment Record, 1938-46, National Archives. http://www.archives.gov.
Santa Barbara News-Press, "Army Graduates Four Local Boys," August 22, 1943.
Santa Barbara News-Press, "From the Fronts," October 18, 1943.
Santa Barbara News-Press, "From the Fronts," March 22, 1944.
Santa Barbara News-Press, "Bob Marxmiller Sent Overseas," April 9, 1944.
Don Olsen (through Ivo de Jong), photo of Schwab Crew, "Box Car," Serial # 42-5262.
U.S. Army Air Force. War Department Missing Air Crew Report #5483, June 11, 1944.
Santa Barbara News-Press, "Missing Man Presumed Dead," June 15, 1943.
Santa Barbara News-Press, "Robert Marxmiller, B-24 Gunner, Is Missing in Action," June 27, 1944.
USAAF Losses. http://www.absa39-45.asso.fr.
World War I, World War II & Korean War Casualty Listing. http://www.ancestry.com.
Honor Roll – 487th Bomb Group. http://www.487BG.org.
487th Bomb Group (H) Station 137 – Lavenham, Suffolk, UK 22-Sep-43 to 7-Nov-45. http://www.487thbg.org.
487th Bomb Group Memorial. http://www.mighty7thaf.preller.us.
Overseas American Cemeteries.
American Battle Monuments Commission.
"In Memoriam," (death of William D. Marxmiller). http://www.sbcfbf.org.

MCALLISTER, EARL ALDER
Dale McAllister (aviator's brother), photos and interview, September 2009.
Olive & Gold, Santa Barbara High School yearbook, 1941.
Santa Barbara News-Press, "R.O.T.C. Cadets Will Visit Camp," May 2, 1941.
Santa Barbara News-Press, "High School Cadets Hold 17th Field Day Program," May 23, 1941.
Santa Barbara News-Press, "Eight More Men Enlist in Navy," August 13, 1942.

Santa Barbara News-Press, "Peggy Hamilton Affianced To Naval Cadet," June 27, 1943.
Santa Barbara News-Press, "Santa Barbarans In Atlantic City," April 11, 1944.
The Ogden Standard-Examiner, "References at Random," April 4, 1945.
Santa Barbara News-Press, "Lt. McAllister Listed Missing," April 12, 1945.
Santa Barbara News-Press, "27 Casualties Listed Last Week," April 15, 1945.
U.S. Casualties of World War II Dead, 1939-1945. http://www.ancestry.com.
"History of USS Bennington World War II Casualties." http://www.uss-bennington.org.

World War II Navy, Marine Corps, and Coast Guard. 1941-1945. http://www.ancestry.com.
"USS Bennington Crew's Stories." http://www.uss-bennington.org.
Veterans with Federal Service Buried in Utah. http://www.familysearch.org.
Chugoku and Shikoku Army Districts. http://www.powresearch.jp.
Navy Department Record, National Archives. http://www.archives.gov.
World War II Honoree, Earl McAllister, honored by Mr. Robert Owen.

MCCLOSKEY, FRED CHADWICK
Olive & Gold, Santa Barbara High School yearbook, 1940.
U.S. World War II Army Enlistment Records, 1938-1946. http://www.ancestry.com.
Santa Barbara News-Press, "Short Honeymoon Spent in North by McCloskeys," October 27, 1943.
Santa Barbara News-Press, "From the Fronts," January 17, 1944.
27th Fighter Squadron. http://www.wikipedia.org.
Santa Barbara News-Press, "Lieut. McCloskey Wins Promotion," January 28, 1945.
Santa Barbara News-Press, "Chad M'Closkey Killed In Action," February 2, 1945.
Santa Barbara News-Press, "Widow of Flier Receives Posthumous Decorations," August 26, 1945.
"Fred McCloskey's Awards," 1st Fighter Group, 27th Squadron. http://www.armyaircorpsmuseum.org.
http://www.1stfighter.com.
World War II Casualties. http://www.kykinfolk.com/adair/ww2casualties.

MESA, NICHOLAS JOHN
John Mesa (aviator's son), photos and interview, January 30, 2010.
Santa Barbara News Press, "Corporal Mesa," June 6, 1943.
Santa Barbara News-Press, "Airman Missing Following Raid," August 25, 1943.
U.S. Army Air Force. War Department Missing Air Crew Report #3748, April 16, 1944.
USAF Aircraft Serial Number, Serial # 42-0129. http://www.cgibin.rcn.com/Jeremy.
U.S. WWII Military Personnel Missing In Action or Lost At Sea, 1941-1946. http://www.ancestry.com.
U.S. Veterans Gravesites, ca.-1775-2006. http://www.ancestry.com.
World War II and Korean Conflict Veterans Interred Overseas. http://www.ancestry.com.
U.S. Rosters of World War II Dead, 1939-1945. http://www.ancestry.com.
Arlington National Cemetery, memorial grave photo. http://www.findagrave.com.
Riverside National Cemetery. http://www.rncsc.org.

MILLER, JOHN EMIL
Ada Bobo (aviator's cousin), letter dated October 26, 2009.
U.S. World War II Army Enlistment Records, 1938-1946. http://www.ancestry.com.
Photo of Kirkland Bombardier Class KT-42-13, 1942, courtesy of Dave Tooley.

Stanford, John V. Jr., photo West Coast Air Force Training Center, Advanced Bombardier School, September 26, 1943.
U.S. Army Air Force. War Department #917, Missing Air Crew Report #917, October 14, 1943.
Kuhl, George C. *"Wrong Place! Wrong Time!" The 305th Bomb Group and the 2nd Schweinfurt Raid, October 14, 1943*, (reviewed by Major M.J. Petersen, USAF in *Air & Space Power Journal*, date unknown).

USAF Serial Number Search, Aircraft Serial # 42-29952, B-17F. http://www.users.rcn.com/Jeremy.k/serial search.
Santa Barbara News-Press, "Pair In Schweinfurt Raid Reported Missing," October 28, 1943.
U.S. Rosters of World War II Dead, 1939-1945. http://www.ancestry.com.
Santa Barbara News-Press, "Four Tri-County Fliers Win Decorations," November 29, 1943.
"Waist Gunner," B-17 Flying Fortress. http://www.b17queenofthesky.com.
"305th Bombardment Group (Heavy)," RAF Chelveston. http://www.en.wikipedia.org.
The 305th Bomb Group War Memorial. http://www.chelveston.org.uk.
Bombardiers of World War II, John E. Miller, 364 BS, 305 BG (H). http://www.freepages.military.rootsweb.ancestry.com.
War Department Files, National Archives & Records Administration. http://www.archives.gov.

MOFFETT, WILLIAM LYNN
Jannell Jenkins & Sherrie Gardner (aviator's nieces), photos.
U.S. World War II Army Enlistment Records, 1938-1946. http://www.ancestry.com.
Unidentified newspaper, "Smoot Bombardier Bags German Fighter Plane," Smoot, Wyoming, (no date), courtesy of Jannell Jenkins and Sherrie Gardner.
Life magazine cover, July 26, 1943.
Santa Barbara News-Press, "Former Santa Barbaran Killed In Crash Following Air Mission," August 2, 1943.
Santa Barbara News-Press, "Moffett Posthumously Honored With 5 Army Air Force Awards," March 26, 1944.
Santa Barbara News-Press, "Gold Star Citations Await Men's Families," June 25, 1944.
U.S. WWII Military Personnel Missing In Action or Lost At Sea, 1941-1946. http://www.ancestry.com.
World War II and Korean Conflict Veterans Interred Overseas. http://www.ancestry.com.
U.S. Army Air Force. War Department Missing Air Crew Report #19649, April 10, 1946.
North Africa American Cemetery and Memorial, American Battle Monuments Commission.
WWI, WWII and Korean War Casualty Listings (David Gandin death). http://www.ancestry.com.

MOLLENHAUER, ARTHUR PAUL
Olive & Gold, Santa Barbara High School yearbook, 1941.
Santa Barbara News-Press, "Load of Navy Recruits Leave For Duty Daily," January 1, 1942.
Santa Barbara News-Press, "Cadet Mollenhauer Sent to Texas," July 18, 1943.
Santa Barbara News-Press, "From the Fronts," February 28, 1944.

Santa Barbara News-Press, "Navy Fighter Pilot Becomes City's 1st Ace," October 18, 1944.
Santa Barbara News-Press, "Father, Wife Of Formosa Ace Proud Of His Record," October 19, 1944.
Santa Barbara News-Press, photo caption, October 22, 1944.
USN Overseas Aircraft Loss List, October 29, 1944. http://www.aviationarcheology.com.
Santa Barbara News-Press, "Mollenhauer, City's First Naval Ace, Reported Missing In Pacific Action," December 7, 1944.
Santa Barbara News-Press, "10 Soldiers, Navy Flier In Week's Casualties," December 10, 1944.
Santa Barbara News-Press, "Mollenhauer, Listed Missing, Gets Navy Cross," February 25, 1945.
Arthur Mollenhauer, Awards and Citations, Bureau of Naval Personnel Information Bulletin No. 337 (April 1945).
U.S. WWII Military Personnel Missing In Action or Lost At Sea, 1941-1946. http://www.ancestry.com.
World War II and Korean Conflict Veterans Interred Overseas. http://www.ancestry.com.
U.S. Rosters of World War II Dead, 1939-1945. http://www.ancestry.com.

Santa Barbara High School Alumni Newsletter, Spring 2009.
USS Intrepid Service Data. http://www.ussintrepid.org.

MOON, FELIX LEE, JR.
Noreen Pond (aviator's sister), photos and interview, August 3, 2009.
U.S. World War II Army Enlistment Records, 1938-1946. http://www.ancestry.com.
Santa Barbara News-Press, "Identify Victims of Perrin Crash," (undated).
Denison Herald, "2 Perrin Airmen Killed In Crash," *(undated).*
Idaho State Journal, "Oklahoma Crash Kills Idahoan," March 9, 1950.
Morning Avalanche, "Two Air Force Fliers Killed In Crash Of Training Plane," March 9, 1950.
Evening Journal, "Two Airmen Killed In Crash In Texas," March 9, 1950.
San Antonio Light, "Crash Kills Pilot, Cadet," March 9, 1950.
Unidentified newspaper, "AF Officers Identify Pair Dead in Crash," (unknown date).
U.S. Army Air Forces. War Department, Report of Major Accident, Accident #50-3-8-4. http://www.aviationarcheology.com.
Carpinteria Cemetery interment.

NEWMAN, ROBERT WILLIAM
Mrs. Virginia Rabuffi (aviator's sister), photo and correspondence dated August 21, 2009.
Olive & Gold, Santa Barbara High School yearbook, 1935.
U.S. Air Corps. War Department, Technical Report of Aircraft Accident Classification Committee, July 19, 1941.
24th Pursuit Group. http://www.wikipedia.org.
Battle of Bataan. http://www.wikipedia.org.
Santa Barbara News-Press, "3 County Casualties Reported," May 4, 1943.
World War II Prisoners of War, 1941-1946, National Archives & Records Administration. http://www.archives.gov.
Defenders of the Philippines. http://www.Philippine-Defenders.lib.wv.us (Informational website about the defense of the Phillipines including the Bataan Death March and the transfer of prisoners on 'Hellships' to prison camps in Asia).

U.S. WWII Military Personnel Missing In Action or Lost At Sea, 1941-1946.
   http://www.ancestry.com.
World War II and Korean Conflict Veterans Interred Overseas. http://www.ancestry.com.
U.S. Rosters of World War II Dead, 1939-1945. http://www.ancestry.com.
War Department Files, National Archives and Records Administration.
   http://www.archives.gov.

OESCHLER, RICHARD JOHN, JR.

Kathleen Shanalec (aviator's daughter), photos.
Olive & Gold, Santa Barbara High School yearbook, 1938.
Phillips, Michael James. "Richard Oeschler," *History of Santa Barbara County*. Chicago: The S.J. Clarke Publishing Company, 1927.
U.S. World War II Army Enlistment Records, 1938-1946. http://www.ancestry.com.
Santa Barbara News-Press, "19 Local Men Are Inducted By Air Corps," April 21, 1942.
Santa Barbara News-Press, "From the Fronts," November 14, 1942.
Santa Barbara News-Press, "Santa Barbarans Exchange Vows In Roswell Field Post Chapel," January 4, 1943.
Santa Barbara News-Press, "Goletan Training For Commission," January 31, 1943.
Santa Barbara News-Press, "Daughter Born to Army Couple," January 27, 1944.
Santa Barbara News-Press, "From the Fronts," July 11, 1944.
U.S. Army Air Force. War Department Missing Air Crew Report #9688, November 11, 1944.
Santa Barbara News-Press, "Flier Missing On China Mission," November 28, 1944.
U.S. World War II Military Personnel Missing In Action or Lost At Sea, 1941-1946.
   http://www.ancestry.com.
USAF Serial Number Search, Aircraft #42-6300. http://www.cgibin.rcn.com.
Paul W. Wordswood, Major, Air Corps confidential correspondence February 19, 1945.
U.S. Rosters of World War II Dead. http://www.ancestry.com.
World War II and Korean Conflict Veterans Interred Overseas. http://www.ancestry.com.
The Official 444th Bombardment Group Association. http://www.444thbg.org.
Dudhkundi Air Field. http://www.wikipedia.org.
World War II Honoree, Richard John Oeschler Jr., honored by Lewis W. Scott Jr., aviator's cousin.

OWENS, WILLIAM THOMAS

Olive & Gold, Santa Barbara High School yearbook, 1941.
Santa Barbara News-Press, "Load of Navy Recruits Leave For Duty Daily," January 1, 1942.
History Of VT-11/VA-12A/VA-115/VFA-115, US Navy Attack Squadron.
   http://www.home.att.net.
Accident report, USMC, 1st Lt. Neal Golphen Williams, pilot, June 8, 1943.
Aircraft Trouble Analysis, U.S. Navy, Bureau of Aeronautics, June 8, 1943.
Santa Barbara News-Press, "'Bill' Owens Reported Missing In Action," June 13, 1943.
Santa Barbara News-Press, "Missing Local Man's Status Is Confirmed," July 3, 1943.
Santa Barbara News-Press, "Son of Local Couple Killed In New Caledonia Crash," August 4, 1943.
Navy Serial Number Search, Aircraft #12406. http://www.cgibin.rcn.com.
Navy Department Files, National Archives and Records Administration.
   http://www.wwiimemorial.com.
WWI, WWII, and Korean War Casualty Listings. http://www.ancestry.com.

World War II Missing In Action or Buried At Sea, Honolulu Memorial, Hawaii. http://www.wwiimemorial.org.
World War II Honoree, William T. Owens, honored by Mr. Robert Owens, brother.

PECK, CLIFFORD JOSEPH
David J. Peck (aviator's nephew), provided story and photos.
Olive & Gold, Santa Barbara High School yearbook, 1937.
Technical Report of Aircraft Accident Classification Committee, May 12, 1942.
Santa Barbara News-Press, "Clifford Peck Killed In Action," August 19, 1943.
Santa Barbara News-Press, "Flier's Medal Given Father," November 1, 1943.

PERES, JOHN (JACK) RICHARD
Olive & Gold, Santa Barbara High School yearbook, 1937.
U.S. World War II Army Enlistment Records, 1938-1946. http://www.ancestry.com.
"Nine Kittyhawks Destroyed Two Japanese D3AVal's Shot Down At Darwin During Japanese Air Raid," February 19, 1942. http://www.ozatwar.com.
Santa Barbara News-Press, "Peres Officially Listed Missing," August 9, 1942.

Santa Barbara News-Press, "Distinguished Service Cross Awarded Lt. Peres, Air Hero," September 8, 1942.
Santa Barbara News-Press, "Body Of Peres Found In Jungle," September 11, 1942.
Fillmore Herald, "Former Residents Receive Medals For Lt. Peres," September 18, 1942.
"Distinguished Service Cross Citation for Jack R. Peres." http://www.militarytimes.com.
Santa Barbara News-Press, "Former Barbareno Wins Service Cross," November 29, 1942.
W.F. Cravens and J.L. Cate, editors. "Loss of Netherlands East Indies," *The Army Air Forces in World War II, volume 1*, page 393, December 5, 1947.
War Department Files, National Archives & Records Administration. http://www.wwiimemorial.org.
U.S. Rosters of World War II Dead, 1939-1945. http://www.ancestry.com.
Santa Barbara Cemetery interment.
Photo of Peres gravestone, Santa Barbara Cemetery. http://www.findagrave.com.

RICKARD, JACK B.
Olive & Gold, Santa Barbara High School yearbook, 1937.
Santa Barbara News-Press, "Goleta Soldier Killed In North Africa Area," May 9, 1943.
Santa Barbara High School Alumni News (Fall, 2008).
War Department Files, National Archives & Records Administration. http://www.wwiimemorial.org.
U.S. Rosters of World War II Dead, 1939-1945. http://www.ancestry.com.
World War II and Korean Conflict Veterans Interred Overseas. http://www.ancestry.com.
American Battle Monuments Comission, North Africa American Cemetery. http://www.abmc.gov.
Overseas American Cemeteries, North Africa American Cemetery.
319th Bombardment Group. http://www.armyaircorpsmuseum.org.
Oyster, Esther. "History of the 319th BOMB GROUP: The Big Tail Birds." http://www.319thbombgroup.com.
The Original 319th Bombardment Group, Martin B-26 Maurauder Man. http://www.b26.com.

Santa Barbara's Fallen Aviators of World War II

ROBERTS, KENNETH E.
Olive & Gold, Santa Barbara High School yearbook, 1940.
Photos courtesy of *Santa Barbara News-Press*, August 19,1944.
U.S. World War II Army Enlistment Records, 1938-1946. http://www.ancestry.com.
Santa Barbara News-Press, "From the Fronts," February 14, 1944.
Santa Barbara News-Press, "From the Fronts," July 27, 1944.
U.S. Army Air Forces War Department, Missing Air Crew Report #7922, August 3, 1944.
Santa Barbara News-Press, "Lieut. Kenneth Roberts Missing on French Front," August 19, 1944.
Santa Barbara News-Press, "Lt. K.E. Roberts Killed at Front," September 21, 1944.
Santa Barbara News-Press, "High Tri-County Casualty List Given," December 3, 1944.
War Department Files, National Archives & Records Administration.
http://www.wwiimemorial.org.
U.S. Rosters of World War II Dead, 1939-1945. http://www.ancestry.com.
World War II and Korean Conflict Veterans Interred Overseas. http://www.ancestry.com.
American Battle Monuments Commission. http://www.abmc.gov.

P-47 Thunderbolt Pilots Association. 366th Fighter Group.
http://www.366fightergroupassoc.org.

SAWYER, CLARENCE ROBERT JR.
Chismahoo, Carpinteria High School yearbook, 1929.
U.S. World War II Army Enlistment Records, 1938-1946. http://www.ancestry.com.
U.S. Army Air Force. War Department, Missing Air Crew Report #14231, April 7, 1945.
Santa Barbara News-Press, "Carpinteria Corporal Reported As Missing," May 12, 1945.
Santa Barbara News-Press, "Cpl. Sawyer Listed Missing," June 6, 1945.
Santa Barbara News-Press, "15 Tri-Countians On Casualty Lists," June 10, 1945.
U.S. Rosters of World War II Dead, 1939-1945. http://www.ancestry.com.
U.S. Veterans Gravesites, ca. 1775-1945. http://www.ancestry.com.
Eric Kreft. http://www.findagrave.com, photo of Jefferson Barracks National Cemetery grave memorial.
"Bombing of Nagoya In World War II." http://www.wikipedia.org.
29th Bomb Group. http://www.29bg.com/crew.

SOTO, STANLEY HOWARD
Olive & Gold, Santa Barbara High School yearbook, 1937.
Santa Barbara News-Press, "From the Fronts," September 3, 1942.
Santa Barbara News-Press, "Resident Ends 'Chute Training," December 11, 1942.
World War II Gyrene dedicated to the U.S. Marine 1941-1945.
http://www.ww2gyrene.org.
Muster Roll of Officers and Enlisted Men of the U.S. Marine Corps, Second Battalion, Twenty-Eighth Marines, Fifth Marine Division from 1 February to 28 February 1945. http://www.ancestry.com.
Santa Barbara News-Press, "We Caught Hell, Writes Soto From Iwo Jima," March 18, 1945.
Santa Barbara News-Press, "Stanley Soto Killed In Action," March 31, 1945.
Santa Barbara News-Press, "2 Brothers Dead In War, 3rd Soto Given U.S. Duty," May 13,1945.
WWI, WWII, and Korean War Casualty Listings. http://www.ancestry.com.

U.S. Rosters of World War II Dead, 1939-1945. http://www.ancestry.com.
Navy Department Files, National Archives & Records Administration. http://www.wwiimemorial.org.
Overseas American Cemeteries, Honolulu Memorial. http://www.wwiimemorial.com.

STINE, BETTY PAULINE
Olive & Gold, Santa Barbara High School yearbook, 1939.
Goleta Valley Leader, "Nephew of Will Rogers Famed Roper," July 22, 1938.
Santa Barbara News-Press, "Miss Betty Stine Learning to Fly," May 23, 1943.
Santa Barbara News-Press, "Santa Barbara Girl Accepted in Ferry Service," September 2, 1943.
U.S. Army Air Forces. Report of Aircraft Accident, February 25, 1944. http://www.aviationarcheology.com.
Santa Barbara News-Press, "Miss Betty Stine, 22, Killed In Air Crash," February 26, 1944.
Dallas Morning News, "WASP Trainee Killed," February 27, 1944.
The Abilene Reporter-News, "Avenger Trainee Killed in Crash," February 27, 1944.
Santa Barbara News-Press, "Rites Set Thursday For Betty Stine," February 29, 1944.
Santa Barbara News-Press, " Military Funeral Held for WASP, Betty Stine," March 3, 1944.
Santa Barbara News-Press, "Gold Star Citations Await Men's Families," June 25, 1944.
Avenger Field aka Sweetwater Army Air Field. http://www.texasescapes.com/worldwarII/Avenger-Field.
Profile of Betty Stine. http://www.wwii-women-pilots.org/WASP KIA.
Profile of Betty Stine. http://www.wingsacrossamerica.us/wasp.
"Betty Stine – Women Aviators." http://www.womenaviators.org.
Santa Barbara Cemetery interment.
Santa Barbara High School Alumni Newsletter (Fall, 2007).

TOMS, GEORGE PARKER
"School History." T*he Lawrenceville School*. http://www.lawrenceville.org.
Time, "Business & Finance, Atlas Corporation," March 9, 1936.
The New York Times, "G. Parker Toms Dies; California Banker," February 4, 1937.
U.S. World War II Army Enlistment Records, 1938-1946. http://www.ancestry.com.
Los Angeles Times, "Wedding Revealed," March 13, 1942.
Santa Barbara News-Press, "Lt. G.P. Toms, Flier, Killed on Western Front," January 19, 1943.
"Shropshire's Casualties and Aircraft Crashes," RAF Commands Forums. http://www.rafcommands.com.
The New York Times, Deaths – Toms – January 20, 1943.
Santa Barbara News-Press, "Parker Toms Killed By Nazis," January 21, 1943.
Technical Report of Aircraft Accident Classification Committee January 23, 1943. http://www.aviationarcheology.com.
U.S. Rosters of World War II Dead, 1939-1945. http://www.ancestry.com.
U.S.Veterans Gravesites, ca. 1775-2006. http://www.ancestry.com.
Eagle Squadrons. http://www.wikipedia.org.
RAF Atcham. http://www.wikipedia.org.

TROUP, JOHN ROBERT
Betty Rowe (aviator's sister) photo and interview, August 18, 2009.
Goleta Valley Leader, "Bob Troup Visits From Marine Base," May 15, 1942.

World War II Navy, Marine Corps, and Coast Guard Casualties, 1941-1945.
   http://www.ancestry.com.
Aircraft Trouble Analysis, Bureau of Aeronautics, U.S. Navy, October 9, 1942.
Goleta Valley Leader, "Bob Troup First Goletan Killed in War Zone," October 16, 1942.
USS Enterprise CV-6 Action Report, November 13-15, 1942.
Naval Department Files, National Archives & Records Administration.
   http://www.wwiimemorial.org.
Santa Barbara News-Press, "Gold Star Citation Await Men's Families," June 25, 1943.
Goleta Valley Leader, "Goletan Honored Posthumously," June 27, 1943.
U.S. Rosters of World War II Dead, 1939-1945. http://www.ancestry.com.
Naval Battle of Guadalcanal. http://www.wikipedia.org.
Goodwin, T/Sgt Hal, U.S. Marine Corps Combat Correspondent, "SCAT! South Pacific Combat Air Transport Thumbs Its Nose At The Zero To Fly Supplies To Nip-Fighting Yanks," The DC3 Aviation Museum (date unknown).
World War II Honoree, John Robert Troup, honored by Elizabeth T. Rowe, twin sister.
Goleta Cemetery interment.

VERHELLE, EDWARD GEORGE
Irma Nagelmann (aviator's sister) photo, correspondence, and interview, August 3, 2009.
Olive & Gold, Santa Barbara High School yearbook, 1939.
Santa Barbara News-Press, "Pilot Classes to Continue," January 23, 1942.
Santa Barbara News-Press, "From The Fronts," November 1, 1943.
Santa Barbara News-Press, "Verhelle Tells Of Life In War Area," March 19, 1944.
Santa Barbara News-Press, "Eddie Verhelle In Alameda," April 23, 1944.
Santa Barbara News-Press, "From the Fronts," June 17, 1944.
M.U.Beebe, Lt. Cdr., U.S. Navy, Commanding Officer, Fighting Squadron Seventeen, letter to Mrs. Nagelmann, May 29, 1945.
Western Union telegram to George Francis Verhelle from Vice Admiral Randal Jacobs, chief of Naval Personnel (June 12, 1945), courtesy of Irma Nagelmann.
Santa Barbara News-Press, "Lt. Edward Verhelle, Navy Pilot, Killed in Pacific Area," June 13, 1945.
Santa Barbara News-Press, "17 Tri-Countians On Casualty Lists," June 17, 1945.
U.S. WWII Military Personnel Missing In Action or Lost At Sea, 1941-1946.
   http://www.ancestry.com.
WWI, WWII, and Korean War Casualty Listings. http://www.ancestry.com.
U.S. Rosters of World War II Dead, 1939-1945. http://www.ancestry.com.
James Forestall, Secretary of the Navy, for the President, citation awarding Gold Star, August 4, 1945.
H.G. Patrick, Captain USN (Ret.), Awards & Medals, letter to Mrs. Nagelmann, August 4, 1945.
A.H. Gray, Acting Commandant, Eleventh Naval District, letter to Mrs. Nagelmann, May 7, 1946.
Santa Barbara News-Press, "Lt. Edward Verhelle Gets Posthumous Naval Citations," (in possession of Irma Nagelmann, no date).
James O. Clifford, Associated Press writer, "Navy Gives Carrier Hornet to Volunteers," *The Daily Transcript,* May 26, 1998.
Navy Department Files, National Archives & Records Administration.
   http://www.archives.gov.

WADE, ALAN LAVERNE
Olive & Gold, Santa Barbara High School yearbook, 1941.

Santa Barbara News-Press, "R.O.T.C. Cadets Will Visit Camp," May 2, 1941.
Santa Barbara News-Press, "Cadet Officers Hold Banquet," November 24, 1941.
U.S. World War II Army Enlistment Records. http://www.ancestry.com.
Santa Barbara News-Press, "Army Corporal Given Barbeque At Parent's Ranch," July 20, 1943.
Santa Barbara News-Press, "Town Chatter," July 23, 1943.
Santa Barbara News-Press, "Barbecue Fetes Wade Boy On Furlough," August 15, 1943.
Santa Barbara News-Press, "Wade Family Holds Reunion At Ranch," August 22, 1943.
Santa Barbara News-Press, "From the Front," December 7, 1943.
Report of Aircraft Accident, Walla Walla, Washington, September 12, 1944. http://www.aviationarcheology.com.
Aviation Archaelogical Investigation & Research. http://www.aviationarcheology.com.
Santa Barbara News-Press, "Corporal Wade Dies In Crash," September 14, 1944.
http://www.b17sam.com, photo.
Washington Death Index, 1940-1996. http://www.ancestry.com.
Walla Walla, Washington Airport. http://www.wallawallaairport.com.
Santa Barbara Cemetery interment.

WILBER, DEAN KENT

Olive & Gold, Santa Barbara High School yearbook, 1938.
U.S. World War II Army Enlistment Records, 1938-1946. http://www.ancestry.com.
Santa Barbara News-Press, "From the Fronts," November 28, 1942.
Field Artillery School, Fort Sill, Oklahoma, Graduation Program, Officer Candidate Class, Number 53, February 25, 1943.
Santa Barbara News-Press, "From the Fronts," July 18, 1944.
U.S. Rosters of World War II Dead, 1939-1945. http://www.ancestry.com.
Santa Barbara News- Press, "Two Tri-County Names Added to Casualty List," September 18, 1945.
World War II and Korean Conflict Veterans Interred Overseas. http://www.ancestry.com.
American Battle Monuments Commission. http://www.abmc.gov.
War Department Files, National Archives & Records Administration. http://www.wwiimemorial.org.
Members of the the 12th Armored Division. http://www.12tharmoredmuseum.com.
Santa Barbara News-Press, Obituary for Sylvia C. Rennie (aviator's wife) October 17, 2003.

YEE, SAM M.

Jeremy Hass, past president Santa Barbara Club, interview, August 16, 2010.
Santa Barbara City Directories, 1936-41.
U.S. World War II Army Enlistment Records, 1938-1946. http://www.ancestry.com.
WWI, WWII, and Korean War Casualty Listings. http://www.ancestry.com.
U.S. World War II Military Personnel Missing In Action or Lost At Sea, 1941-1946. http://www.ancestry.com.
American Battle Monuments Commission, The World War II Honor Roll
War Department Files, National Archives & Records Administration. http://www.wwiimemorial.org.
McNaughton, James C., Command Historian, Defense Language Institute, Foreign Language Center, Presidio of Monterey "Chinese-Americans in World War II,' May 16, 2000.

INDEX

100th Bomb Group, 26
111th Observation Squadron, 76
11th Air Force, 60, 61
11th Bomb Group, 24, 28
1258th Engineer Combat Battalion, 48
12th Air Force, 76
12th Armored Division, 98
13th Air Force, 58
13th Command Army Air Force, 16, 17
14th Air Force, 52
15th Air Force, 10
19th Bomb Group, 11, 12, 18
1st Fighter Group, 58
23rd Fighter Group, 30
24th Pursuit Group (Navy), 70
250th Field Artillery Group, 98
28th Bomb Group, 60
29th Bomb Group, 4, 84, 85
2nd Marine Aircraft Group, 46
303rd Bomb Group, 9
305th Bomb Group, 22, 62
308th Bomb Group, 52
319th Bomb Group, 80, 81
31st Bombardment Association, 17
366th Fighter Group, 82
392nd Bomb Group, 50
3rd Army, 48
444th Bomb Group, 72, 73
456th Bomb Group, 10
487th Bomb Group, 14, 54, 55
503rd Parachute Infantry Regiment, 40
5th Bomb Group (Heavy), 16, 17, 28
8th Army Air Force, 9, 62, 91
8th Pursuit Group Far East Air Force, 78

A
"Afrika Corps", 76
Adams Refinishing Shop, 3
Adams, Claude McAllister, 2, 3

Adams, Clyde, v, xiv, 2, 3
Adams, Lillian Sophia, 2, 3
Admiral Farragut Academy, New Jersey, 70
Air Corps Gunnery School, Arizona, 96
Air Medal, 9, 16, 17, 23, 25, 28, 29, 37, 47, 55, 58, 61, 63, 65, 67, 73, 77, 95
Alamogordo Army Air Field, New Mexico, 54
Aleutian Campaign, 60
Alexandria Louisiana Navigator School, 72
American Cemetery, Cambridge, England, 15
American Cemetery, Italy, 77
American Cemetery, Margraten, Netherlands, 9
American Cemtery, Fort Bonifacio, Manila, Philippines, 17, 19, 29
American Defense Medal, 12
American St. Laurent, France, 83
Arlington National Cemetery, 61
Army Air Force XX Command, 72, 73
Army Air Forces Training Command, South Dakota, 96
Arnold, Dean Alden, v, 4, 5
Arnold, Ethel Mae, 4
Arnold, Kenneth, 4, 5
Arnold, Price Younger, 4
Asian Theater, xiii, 12
Asia-Pacific Campaign Medal, 95
Asiatic-Pacific Theater Service Campaign Ribbon, 53
AT-6 Texan, 88
Atchem Air Field, England, 91
Avenger Field, Arizona, 88

B
B-17 Flying Fortress, 8, 10, 14, 18, 22, 24, 26, 28, 31, 54, 62, 63, 96
B-24 Liberator, xiv, 10, 14, 24, 36, 37, 50, 52, 53, 54, 60, 64, 65, 72

B-26 Widowmaker, 80
B-29 Superfortress, 4, 12, 24, 54, 65, 72, 73, 84
Bartow, Florida, 30
Bar-U, 50
Bataan Death March, 71
Bates, Bertha Lee, 6
Bates, Fred, 6
Bates, Kenneth, 6
Bates, Philip, v, xiv, 6
Bates, Thomas Wheatley, 6
Battle of Midway, 32
Battle of Mindoro, 40
Battle of Tarawa, 21
Battle of the Solomons, 36
Becknell, Edna Mae, 8, 9
Becknell, Harry Eugene, 8
Becknell, Herman, 8
Becknell, Wallace Earl, v, 8, 9
Bernberg Air Field, Germany, 50
Biak (South Pacific), 16
Bigelow, John A., 52
Black Sheep Squadron, 46
Boggs, Mary Jane, 28
Boss Lady, 26
Botello, Erlinda, 10
Botello, Francis L., v, 10, 11
Botello, Maclovio, 10
Botello, Virginia, 10
Box Car, 54, 55
Boyington, Marine Major Pappy, 46
Bozorth, Ralph, 89
Brittany American Cemetery, St. James, France, 55
Bronze Oak Leaf Cluster, 58
Bronze Star, 87
Brown Military Academy, California, 96
Bruning Army Air Field, Nebraska, 14
BT-11 Torpedo Squadron, 74
Burns, Katie Ann, 12, 13
Burns, Mary Ellen (Putnam), xiii, 12, 13
Burns, Jr., James Edward, v, xiii, 12, 13
Butler, Mary Lou (Marie), 16
Buttfield, William, 85

C

Caddo Mills Cemetery, Texas, 9
Cal Poly San Luis Obispo, California, 92
Cal Tech, Pasadena, California, 42, 52
Calvary Cemetery, Santa Barbara, 21, 77
Camp Gruber, Oklahoma, 98

Camp McCain, Mississippi, 96
Camp Pendleton, San Diego, California, 92
Camp Roberts, California, 98
Camp Walters, Texas, 96
Canadian Air Force, 2
Carlson, Bob, 82
Carman (Carmen), Earnest Darrel, v. xiii, 14. 15
Carman, Clara Starr , xiii, xiv, 14, 15
Carman, Elbert Levi, 14, 15
Carman, Violet, 15
Carney Field, Guadalcanal, 28
Carpinteria Cemetery, 6, 68, 85
Carpinteria Community Church, 6
Carpinteria High School, xiii, 6, 39, 42, 45, 68, 84
Carpinteria High School World War II Memorial, 63, 85
Carpinteria Valley Post of the Veterans of Foreign Wars, 45
Carson, Dewey, 16
Cass Field, Philippines, 17
Cass, Emery, 16, 17
Cass, Gerald, v, xiii, 16, 17
Cass, Helen, 16
Cass, Ruth Ellen, 16, 17
Caught in the Draft, 9
Chapman, Barbara, 52, 53
Charbonneau, Lawrence G., 82
Clark Air Field, Philippines, 70
Clark, Edna Mae, 8, 9
Coffman, Mary Alice, xv
College of the Pacific, 38
Colt, Frances (Nan) Bacon, 32, 33
Cook Sr., Cecil Palrang, 18
Cook, Bill, 18
Cook, Jim, 18
Cook, Jr., Cecil Palrang, v, xiv, 18, 19
Cook, Margaret (Stapleton), 18
Corsair F4U, 46
Cortez, Lawrence, 57
Courville, Earl A., v, xi, xiv, 20, 21
Courville, Herbert, 20
Courville, Louis, 20
Courville, Mary Juanita, 20
Coverstone, Dale, 22
Coverstone, Dean, 22
Coverstone, Ethel Hendricks, 22
Coverstone, Lanar, 22
Coverstone, Robert E., v, 22, 23
Coverstone, Virgil, 22
Craig Field, Alabama, 76
Crego, Remsen H.R., 6

D

Da Vinci, Leonardo, xv
Darling, Major Henry B., 3
Darnell, Lt., 51
Davao Penal Colony (Philippines), 18
Davis, Radio Sgt., 29
Day, Silvia C. (Wilber), 98
de la Guerra y Noriega, Jose Antonio, 24
De Roo, Cpl. Raymond, 25
De Seversky, Alexander, 70
Democratic National Convention, xiii
Dibblee, Anita Orena, 24
Dibblee, Francis Richard, v, 24, 25
Dibblee, T. Wilson, 24
Distinguished Flying Cross, 12, 17, 37, 65, 95
Distinguished Service Cross, 78, 79
Donaldson, John Louis, v, xv, 26, 27, 35
Donaldson, Marion Harding, 26
Donaldson, William, 26
Donaldson, George, xv, 26, 27
Doolittle, General Jimmy, 26
Du Bois, William, 13
Dudhkundi Air Field, India, 72
Dwight Murphy Field, Santa Barbara, 17

E

East Texas Teachers College, 8
Eckles, Berthel (Bert), 28
Eckles, Howard, 28, 29
Eckles, Mattie (Smith), 28
Eckles, Rex, I, v, xi, 28, 29
Eglin Field, Florida, 2
Elings Park County Veterans Terrace of Remembrance, 39, 95
European Theater, xiii
Exclusion Act, 100

F

F4F Wildcat, xiv, 44
F6F Hellcat, 46, 56, 66
Fagan, Lawrence, 90
Farmersville High School, Texas, 8
Fennell, Virginia (Sawyer), 84
Fertig, Brigadier Wendell, 19
Field Artillery Officers' Candidate School, Oklahoma, 98
Fifth Marine Division, 86, 87
Fighting Squadron (VF-18), 67
Fighting Squadron 17, 95
Fighting Squadron 6, 42
Fighting Squadron 82, 56
Firestone, Evelyn (Kohen), 30
Firestone, Gerald, 30, 31
Firestone, Irving, 30
Firestone, Norman Selwyn, v, xiii, 30, 31, 92
Flying Boxcar, 10
Fort Belvoir, Virginia, 48
Fort Benning, Georgia, 40
Fort Bliss, Texas, 97
Fort Lewis, Washington, 20
Fort Sumner, New Mexico, 24, 26
Fort William McKinley Monument, Manila, Phillipines, 33, 47, 67, 71, 73, 87
Fortress Corregidor, 40
Fowler, James Laurence, I, v, xi, xiii, 32, 33
Fowler, Laurence, 32
Fowler, Margaret (McDonald), 32
Fox, Naval Lt., 29
Franco, Nicholas John, 60

G

Gandin, Dave, 64, 65
Garcia, Esperenza, 60
Gardner Field, Taft, California, 22
Gardner, Sherrie, 64
Garfield Elementary School, Santa Barbara, California, 76
Goethe, Lt. Everett F., 14
Gold Star, 95
Golden Gate Cemetery, San Francisco, California, 91
Goleta Cemetery, 58, 93
Govern Field, Idaho, 4
Granite Rock, Riverside Co., California, 34
Grasshopper Observation Plane, 98
Great Depression, iii
Greene, Ass. Enj. Sgt., 29
Griggs, Bernice, 34
Griggs, Jr., Augustus Monroe, v, xiv, 34
Griggs, Sarah Dodsworth, 34
Griggs, Sr., Augustus, 34
Griggs, Sue Ann, 34
Grosse Isle Michigan Naval Reserve Air Base, 42
Grumman TBF/TBM Avenger, 74
Guam, 4, 5, 12

H

Halsey, Commander, 43
Hamilton, Margaret (Peggy) (McAllister), 56, 57
Hancock College of Aeronautics, Santa Maria, California, 24
Hancock Field, Santa Maria, California, 72, 82
Harmon Field, Guam, 24
Harmon, Lt. General Millard F., 28
Harshbarger, Barbara, 34
Harshbarger, Dr. Miller, 36
Harshbarger, Grace Campbell, 36
Harshbarger, William, xiv
Harshbarger, William Miller, v, xiv, 36, 37
Hartley, Cyril Owen, v, xiii, xiv, 38, 39
Hartley, Daisy Ripken, 38, 39
Hawthorne Field, North Carolina, 26
Hays, Florence Peterson, 40, 41
Hays, Jerry, 41
Hays, John William, v, xiii, xiv, 40, 41
Hays, Kenneth, 40
Hays, William Washington, 40
Hebel, Francis Frederick, v, xiv, xv, 42-45
Hebel, Frank, 42
Hebel, Wilhelmina Loga, 42
Hendrix, Homer Lloyd, 73
Hendrix, Melinda, 73
Hengyang Air Field, China, 30
Hewston, Emmett, 40
Hickam Field, Hawaii, 36, 44
Hill, 29
Hirt, Gretchen (Oeschler), 72
HMS Glory, 33
Hoffman, Harrell Ringo, 60
"The Hump", 73

I

Irvine, Wilda, xv
Irwin, Louise E. (Keister), 46

J

Jefferson Barracks National Cemetery, 5, 11, 85
Jeschke, Col. R. H., 33
Jones, Lt., 29

K

Kahili Air Field, Bougianville, 28, 29
Kara Field, Solomon Islands, 46
Keister, Lanorah Hands, 46
Keister, Robert Louis, v, 46, 47
Keister, Thaddeus L., 46
Kelly Field, Texas, 38, 54, 78
Kelly, Sgt. Enj., 29
King, Enid L., 22
Knapp, Mary Ellen, 83
Knop, Bombardier Lt., 29
Knowles, Bill, 37
Knowles, David, 37
Knowles, Sally, 37
Kochi Air Field (Shikoku), Japan, 57
Krempuach, Andrew F., 60
Kurtz, Edna Grace, 16
Kwanghan Air Field, China, 73

L

La Cumbre Junior High (Santa Barbara), California, 76
La Flamme Photography Studio, 20
La Flamme, Alice, 20
La Flamme, Betty, 20
La Flamme, Frank, 20
Laguna Blanca School, 24
Lassen High School, California, 14
Lassen Junior College, California, 14
Laurinberg-Maxton Army Air Base, North Carolina, 21
Lavenham, England, 14, 54
Lawrenceville Preparatory School, New Jersey, 90
LeMay, Curtis, 84
Lichty, Phil, 22
Liege, Belgium, 14
Life magazine, 64
Lil' Nell, 29
Lockheed Aircraft, 2, 78
Long Beach Naval Station, 6
Lopez, Canadalaria Alvararo, 48
Lopez, Consuelo Linda, 48
Lopez, Daniel V., 48
Lopez, Frederick Peter, I, v, xi, 48, 49
Lopez, James, 48
Lopez, Jose, 48
Lorraine American Cemetery, St. Avoid, France, 48, 99
Love, David Culver, v, 50, 51
Love, Harold, 50

Love, Mildred Culver, 50
Lowe, Lt. John K., 24
Lowry Field, Colorado, 10, 54
Lubbock Army Flying School, Texas, 16
Lucas, Anthony Dean, 29
Lucas, Gwendolyn, 29
Lucas, Rex, 29
Luke Field, Arizona, 36, 82
Luliang Air Field, China, 30, 53
Lundstrom, John B., 43, 44

M
MacDill Field, Florida, 4
MacDougall, Ensign A., 6
MacFarland, Andrew Bruce (Andy), xiv, 53
MacFarland, Andrew Ransalier, v, xiv, 52, 53, 58
MacFarland, Ransalier, 52
MacFarland, Ruth, 52
Marana Air Field, Arizona, 22
March Air Field, Riverside Co., California, 36, 77
Marine Corps Air Station, Santa Barbara, xi, 32, 46
Marxmiller, Chester, 54, 55
Marxmiller, Irma Mae Smithley, 54, 55
Marxmiller, Robert K., v, 54, 55
Marxmiller, William David, 54, 55
Mary Lou, 16
Mather Air Base, California, 28, 38
McAllister, Dale, xiv
McAllister, Earl Alder, v, xv, 56, 57
McAllister, John Wells, 56
McAllister, Linda, 57
McAllister, Mary Meryl, 56
McCloskey, Dorothy Tinker, 58
McCloskey, Fred , 58
McCloskey, Fred Chadwick, v, 58, 59
Mecham, Nancy, 20
Mediterrean Theater, iii
Meisler, Philip S., 67
Menges, Ensign Herbert H., 44
Mesa, Frank, 60
Mesa, John Anthony, xiv, 60, 61
Mesa, Nicholas John , v, xiv, 60, 61
Miller, Benjamin, 62
Miller, John Emil, v, 62, 63
Miller, Marguerite Cone, 62
Milliken, William M., 50
Minter, John H., 81
Mitscher, Mark, 56

Model T, 50
Moffett, Leander, 64
Moffett, Leonard, xiii, 64
Moffett, Rose, 64
Moffett, Rose Gomm, 64
Moffett, William Lynn, vi, xiii, 64, 65
Molesworth Air Station, England, 9
Mollenhauer, Arthur Paul, vi, 66, 67
Mollenhauer, Augusta Kuglitsch, 66
Mollenhauer, Clarence, 66
Mollenhauer, Jr., Paul, 66
Mollenhauer, Paul, 66
Mollenhauer, Robert, 66
Moon, Jr., Felix Lee, vi, xiii, xiv, 68
Moon, Marjorie Hansen, 68
Moon, Noreen, 68
Moon, Sr., Felix Lee, 68
Murdock, Douglas L., 63
Muroc Air Field (Edwards Air Force Base), California, 34, 50, 52
Musser, John L., 5
My Achin' B, 22, 23

N
Nagelmann, Irma, xv
National Cemetery, Ardennes, France, 51
National Memorial Cemetery of the Pacific, Honolulu, HI, 25, 45, 61, 74, 87, 94, 95
Naval Air Station (Pasco), Washington, 66
Naval Air Training Center, Corpus Christi, Texas, 32, 66
Navy Cross Medal, 67
Navy Pier (Chicago), Illinois, 66
Neuville-En-Condroz Permanent Cemetery, Belgium, 51
New Brittain, Papua, New Guinea, 32
Newman, Betty, 70
Newman, Frances Gill, 70
Newman, Marian, 70
Newman, Robert William, vi, xiv, 70, 71
Newman, Rolla (Raul), 70
Newman, Virginia, 70, 71
Normandy American Cemetery, 83
North Africa Campaign, 80
North African American Cemetery & Memorial (Tunsia), 65, 81

O
Oak Leaf , 17, 65
O'Brien, Bill, 95

Occidental College, Los Angeles, 6
Oeschler, Elsie, 72
Oeschler, Jr., Richard, vi, xiv, 72, 73
Oeschler, Kathleen (Shenalec), xiv, 73
Oeschler, Sr., Richard, 72
Ontario Army Air Field, California, 65
Operation Husky, 77
Oujda Air Field, Morrocco, 81
Owens, Anne Thomas, 74
Owens, Myrick, 74
Owens, Robert, 75
Owens, William Thomas, vi, 74, 75
Oxnard High School, 40

P

P-35, 70, 71
P-38 Lightning, iii, 34, 58
P-39 Airacobra, 20, 76, 77, 91
P-40 Warhawk, 30, 78
P-47 Thunderbolt, 46, 82
P-51 Mustang, iii, 30, 77
Pacific Theater, xi, xiii, 2, 16, 53, 54, 72, 92
Paramushiru (Kamchatka Pennisula), 60
Parker, Bessie, 90
Pearl Harbor, xiii, 2, 14, 36, 38, 42, 44, 70
Peck, Bertha S., 76
Peck, Clifford Joseph, vi, 76, 77
Peck, David J., 76
Peck, Edgar L., 76
Peck, Len, 76
Peck, Ruth, 40, 41
Peres, Herman, 79
Peres, Jack, I, vi, xi, 78, 79
Peres, John, 78
Peres, Leona, 78
Peres, Louise (Buch), 78
Perrin Field, (Air Force Base), Texas, 39, 68
Peterson, First Lieutenant Lawrence, 10
Philippines Campaign, 86
Phillips, Lieutenant, 82
Pomona College, California, 32
Pope Pius XII, 58
Purple Heart, 9, 12, 15, 17, 19, 25, 29, 47, 48, 51, 53, 55, 61, 65, 67, 73, 77, 78, 79, 83, 87, 95, 100
Pyle, Ernie, 45

R

R4D-F Marine Corps Transport airplane, 74

Randolph Field, Texas, 16, 38
Rennie, John, 99
Rickard, George, 80
Rickard, Irma (Burleson), 80
Rickard, Jack B., vi, xiv, 80, 81
Rickard, Roy F., 80
Riverside National Cemetery, California, 61
Roberts, Kenneth E., vi, 82, 83
Roberts, Phillip, 82
Roberts, Sara (Menning), 82
Rogers, Will, 88
Rommel, Erwin, 76
Roosevelt, Franklin D., xiii
Roswell Bombadier School, 72
Royal Air Force (Canada), 90
RP-38 IE, 34
Ryan-Hemet Air Field, Riverside Co., California, 34

S

Salinas Air Field, California, 37
San Diego Marine Base, California, 46
Santa Ana Army Air Base (SAAAB), California, 4, 22, 24, 30, 34, 52, 72, 82
Santa Barbara Airport, I, xi, xiii, xiv, 3, 5, 9, 13, 17, 19, 29, 31, 33, 34, 39, 47, 49, 51, 55, 59, 65, 67, 76, 83, 87
Santa Barbara Cemetery, 34, 53, 63, 79, 89, 95, 97
Santa Barbara Club, 100
Santa Barbara High School, xiii, 4, 5, 18, 20, 22, 26, 27, 28, 30, 32, 34, 36, 38, 39, 50, 52, 53, 54, 56, 58, 59, 66, 70, 71, 72, 74, 76, 78, 79, 80, 82, 84, 86, 88, 94, 96, 97, 98
Santa Barbara High School World War II Memorial, 5, 27, 29, 31, 33, 53, 59, 71, 75, 97
Santa Barbara State College, 24, 28, 38, 52, 54, 64, 72, 78, 79, 84, 94
Sawyer, Carrie Phelps, 84, 85
Sawyer, Jr., Clarence Robert, vi, 42, 84, 85
Sawyer, Robert Fennell, 84
Sawyer, Sr., Clarence Robert, 84
Sawyer, Virginia (Fennell), 85
Schmitz, Jacqueline (Toms), 90
Schwab, Floyd, 54
Shedd, William, 58
Shinyo Maru, 18, 19
Shoemaker, Capt. James M., 44
Silver Oak Leaf Cluster, 17

Silver Star Medal, 57
Simpson Harbor, Rabual, 32, 33
Sizzle, 62, 63
Slebiss, Ilone, 60
Smith, Herman F., 73
Snow, Bernard, 63
Soto, Bernard, xiv, 86
Soto, Francis, xiv, 86, 87
Soto, Josie, 86
Soto, Peter J., 86
Soto, Stanley Howard, vi, xiv, 86, 87
Soto, Susan J., 86
St. Mary's College, Moraga, California, 32
Steed, Colonel Thomas W., 10
Steed's Flying Colts, 10
Stevens, Marilee, 50
Stillman, Don, 50
Stine, Betty, I, vi, xi, xiii, xiv, 88, 89
Stine, Jake, 88
Stine, Mary Allen, 88
Stornara Field, Italy, 10

T

T-6, 68
Tablets of the Missing, East Coast Memorial, New York, 100
Taboo, 10, 11
Task Force 58, 56
Taylorcraft Grasshopper, xiii
TBF-1 Avenger, 32
Tenney, Marianne, 96
Texas A & M, 70
The First Team; Pacific Naval Air Combat from Pearl Harbor to Midway, 43
The Spearhead, 87
The Temptation, 24, 25
The Turkey, 74
Thurleigh Field, England, 23
Tokyo Taxi, 28, 29
Toms, Jr., George Parker, vi, 90
Toms, Marion Fagan, 90
Toms, Sr., George Parker, 90
Toms, Wendy, 91
Tontota Air Field, New Caledonia, 74
Torokina Air Field, Bougainville, 32
Torres, Consuelo (Lopez), 48
Townsend, Sally, 36
Troup, Jeannie (Main), 92
Troup, Jeannie Elizabeth (Betty), 92, 93
Troup, John, 92
Troup, John Robert (Bobbie), vi, 92, 93

Troup, William (Gordon), 92
Turner Field, Georgia, 26

U

University of Arizona, 88
University of California, 90
University of California, Berkeley, 30, 82, 84
University of California, Davis, 28, 36
University of California, Los Angeles, 12, 78
University of Colorado Law School, 16
University of Hawaii, 72
University of Wyoming, 64
USAT Dorchester, 100
USS Bennington, 56, 57
USS Enterprise, 42, 56
USS Hornet, 94, 95
USS Intrepid, 66, 67
USS Lexington, 56
USS Paddle, 18

V

Verhelle, Angela Cartieri, 94
Verhelle, Edward George, vi, xiii, xv, 94, 95
Verhelle, George, 94
Verhelle, Irma, 94
Verhelle, Yvonne, 94
VF-6, 43, 44
Victorville Bomber School, California, 64
Vigue, Harold L., 25
VT-11 Torpedo Squadron, 74
VT-13 A Valiant, 38
Vth Marine Amphibious Corps, 87

W

Wade, Alan LaVerne, vi, xiv, 96, 97
Wade, Jr., Martin Peter, 96, 97
Wade, Matilda (Molly) Altenburg, 96
Wade, Sr., Martin Peter, 96
Walla Walla Air Field, Washington, 37
WASP World War II Women, 89
Weidner, Eleanor, 66
Welsh, Peggy Lou (McAllister), 58
Wessinger, Ray Alan, 53
Wessinger, Ray Andrew, 53
Wheeler Field, Hawaii, 44
White, Captain Gerald A., 9
White, Lt. Morgan, 82, 83
Wilber, Cornelia Kent, 98

Wilber, Dean Kent, vi, xiv, 98, 99
Wilber, Deanna, 98
Wilber, Glenn, 98, 99
Wilber, James, 98
Wilber, Ruth, 98
Wilber, Sylvia (Day), 99
Will Rogers Field, Oklahoma, 4
Williams Field, Arizona, 2, 22, 34
Williams, Neal G., 74
Witmer, Alexis , 23
Witmer, Marie, 23
Women Airforce Service Pilots (WASP), 88, 89
Women's Air Ferrying Service, 88
World War II Memorial, Santa Barbara High School, 4, 25, 28, 32, 70, 96
World War II Victory Medal, 95

Y

Yamato (Japanese Warship), 56
Yee, Sam M., vi, xiii, 100

www.ingramcontent.com/pod-product-compliance
Lightning Source LLC
Chambersburg PA
CBHW081133170426
43197CB00017B/2848